The Bedford Guide
for Writing Tutors

The Bedford Guide for Writing Tutors

Sixth Edition

Leigh Ryan
University of Maryland, College Park

Lisa Zimmerelli
Loyola University Maryland

Bedford/St. Martin's
A Macmillan Education Imprint

Boston • New York

For Bedford/St. Martin's

Vice President, Editorial, Macmillan Higher Education Humanities: Edwin Hill
Editorial Director, English and Music: Karen S. Henry
Senior Publisher for Composition, Business and Technical Writing, Developmental Writing: Leasa Burton
Executive Editor: Karita France dos Santos
Developmental Editors: Rachel Childs, Evelyn Denham
Production Assistant: Erica Zhang
Publishing Services Manager: Andrea Cava
Production Supervisor: Carolyn Quimby
Project Management: DeMasi Design and Publishing Services
Director of Rights and Permissions: Hilary Newman
Text Design: DeMasi Design and Publishing Services
Cover Design: William Boardman
Composition: Achorn International, Inc.
Printing and Binding: RR Donnelley and Sons

Manufactured in the United States of America.

0 9 8 7 6
f e d c b

For information, write: Bedford/St. Martin's, 75 Arlington Street, Boston, MA 02116
(617-399-4000)

ISBN 978-1-4576-5072-7

Preface for Writing Center Directors

In my early years of directing a university writing center, I longed for a single, short book that my tutors and I could learn from, one that could serve as a resource for tutoring information and techniques. Though I wasn't trying to make composition teachers out of engineering or psychology or dance majors, I did want the tutors to acquire some knowledge of the writing process as well as some strategies that they could use as they worked with writers. Because the book didn't exist, I gathered articles and excerpts that we read and discussed. I created and borrowed assignments and exercises to help tutors learn and practice skills. And, I tried to create an environment in which we could share our experiences and learn from one another.

Writing the first edition of *The Bedford Guide for Writing Tutors* gave me the chance to create that short book, one that discusses how tutoring fits into the writing process; offers tutors suggestions and strategies to help writers improve their writing; and discusses specific kinds of writers, situations, and assignments that tutors are apt to encounter. It invites tutors to examine and consider their tutoring roles, and it reminds them that they are professionals who are working with writers. Subsequent editions allowed for refining information, adding assignments and activities, acknowledging the growth of writing centers globally and in secondary schools, and including discussions about the increasing impact of technology on writing and tutoring.

With the fourth edition, I asked my former assistant director Lisa Zimmerelli to collaborate with me. An outstanding teacher, administrator, and tutor—both face-to-face and online—her thoughtful and wise contributions have been invaluable. Our collaboration often resembles a tutoring session as we pose questions for each other about our audience, purpose, content, phrasing, and word choices. With each edition, working with Lisa reminds me anew of Kenneth Bruffee and the social nature of tutoring.[1]

Recent editions of *The Bedford Guide for Writing Tutors* reflect the ever-increasing impact of technology on writing, tutoring, and learning. The sixth edition addresses the intersection of tutoring and technology more fully and incorporates suggestions for best practices in synchronous online tutoring throughout. We also carefully edited this edition with an eye toward the growing international and secondary communities of writing centers—both very exciting phenomena—and added a chapter, "Research in the Writing Center," to encourage and support the professional development of tutors.

---

[1] Kenneth Bruffee. "Collaborative Learning and the 'Conversation of Mankind.'" *College English* 46 (November 1984): 635–52.

Moreover, because this book is used on six of the seven continents (we know of no writing center in Antarctica!), and in multiple kinds of educational contexts, including secondary schools, we have been mindful of including examples and tutor scenarios that represent this expansion. The wide variety of explanations, examples, and exercises acknowledges, reflects, and respects the practices and concerns of the diverse populations within writing centers found across institutions and cultures. Some areas of inquiry are of special interest to a geographic area, and we were mindful of that as we wrote. In the United States, for example, the issue of students' right to their own language is an important and significant topic. Because that may not be the case in other countries, we opted not to address it directly here.

Similarly, issues around gender, race, ethnicity, religion, class, sexuality, and physical ability will inevitably arise in a writing center, and the available responses to these issues vary greatly among cultures. A general, short text such as *The Bedford Guide for Writing Tutors* cannot adequately cover all possible situations and issues, and so we invite you to explore more deeply with your tutors the concerns or subjects that affect the writers who visit your writing center.

As a way of judging how the writing center is operating at any given time, we listen to the general buzz—that hum—as tutors and writers work together. The gauge is laughter. In the midst of the serious business of discussing content, organization, documentation, and rules for semicolons, those audible expressions of enjoying what they are doing tell us *loudly* that all is well. Our hope is that the tone of *The Bedford Guide for Writing Tutors* reflects the professional yet friendly tone we expect of tutors, and that the occasional cartoon underscores that by provoking a smile or chuckle.

How to Use This Guide

We believe that writing center administrators everywhere will find this book useful. Staff, clients, services, and missions vary from one writing center to another. We hope that administrators will adapt this guide to the unique needs of their writing centers, spending more or less time on specific sections and appropriate exercises and supplementing with articles, handouts, and exercises they may already use. But *The Bedford Guide for Writing Tutors* first and foremost offers advice and suggestions to writing tutors. Reviewers and users continually acknowledge its brevity and practicality as its chief virtues, even as they sometimes request more content in some areas.

Most of us—administrators and tutors—view writing centers through the lens of what we know. Not surprisingly, that's our own writing centers. Just listen to presenters at conferences—directors and tutors alike—as they discuss a writing course called "English 108," assuming that listeners will know what they mean, or refer to "Writing Central" or the "Café"—the name of their writing center—as if everyone will automatically recognize that as the writing center.

Writing centers do vary, and significantly. Some offer only face-to-face sessions; others provide only online tutoring, which may be synchronous, asynchronous, or a blend of the two; and some offer a mix of face-to-face and online tutoring. Staff may be peer tutors, graduate students, professional tutors, faculty, or even community volunteers, and the population served is typically unique to a writing center's particular college or institution: undergraduates, graduate students, faculty, staff, community writers, or some combination thereof. Services include not only tutoring but also workshops, grammar hot-lines, chats, and online files of handouts. Hours vary, with services available days, evenings, or even on weekends. Locations for sessions—for example, classrooms, libraries, or dormitories—vary as well.

The Bedford Guide for Writing Tutors intends to be a general guide for writing tutors across the spectrum of writing centers—face-to-face and online. Furthermore, while its main focus may be writing center tutors, it attempts to accommodate individual tutors as well. Since particular institutions serve specific populations, we encourage you to supplement the guide with readings and online resources that focus on the needs of your clients.

What also varies, and significantly, is tutor training, and for that reason we have tried to provide a wide variety of exercises. Our hope is to accommodate large classes of twenty and small classes of one or two, as well as tutors at large state universities, small private institutions, community colleges, and secondary schools. The exercises in this guide connect directly with acquiring and practicing tutoring skills and strategies. Many training programs require tutors to maintain a journal or participate in online conversations, so we've included suggestions for those activities. We've also included typical assignments in which tutors investigate and discuss their own writing processes. Because some new tutors haven't been tutored themselves, we suggest that they seek tutoring as they complete the assignment. Other exercises ask tutors to investigate how writing is taught at their school as well as to practice and discuss tutoring tools and strategies. Later activities ask tutors to reflect on and synthesize their tutoring experiences. For use with larger classes, some exercises include many options; if your class is small, you might limit those options by asking tutors to go through only a few of the exercises. We invite you to choose, rearrange, adapt, and tailor these exercises to your needs and those of your writing center. You might, for example, choose to ask tutors to complete some exercises before reading a chapter in order to get them thinking about issues and to give them a reason to read more carefully.

Because tutors work with writers rather than just with papers, we include no complete sample texts of student writing. While tutors could discuss how they might begin a session with a particular paper or what they might focus on, without a writer to respond, tutors can only speculate—an arrangement that does not represent the reality of a tutoring session. We also believe that discussing how isolated papers might be improved encourages tutors to correct the writing rather than to ask the questions that will guide the writer to a better understanding of the composition process.

Acknowledgments

For this edition, we turned to several colleagues for advice and suggestions, and we are grateful to them for their wisdom and guidance: Ted Roggenbuck, Bloomsburg University; Jared Featherstone, James Madison University; Amber Jensen, Edison High School; and Isabell May, University of Baltimore.

Thanks, too, to the late Diana Hacker for her wisdom, guidance, and support. A special note of thanks to Colleen Ryan Leonard, Matt Ryan, and John Zimmerelli, each of whom patiently listened, read, and advised through drafts. Lisa wishes to acknowledge the understanding of her three children, Carmine, Hildegard, and Roberta, who shared their Mommy with this book many a weekend.

Thanks again to those at Bedford/St. Martin's: Leasa Burton, Karita France dos Santos, Rachel Childs, and Evelyn Denham. We are also grateful to Erica Zhang and Linda DeMasi, who carefully oversaw the production of the sixth edition, and to Nancy Crompton for her skillful copyediting.

Most especially, Leigh wishes to acknowledge and thank her assistant directors, former and current: Rebecca Spracklin, Charles Magnetti, Francis DeBernardo, Melinda Schwenk, Jenny Steinberg, Traci Abbott, Rachel Kovacs, Patricia Lissner, Eleanor Shevlin, Greg Wahl, Sara Glasgow, Elliot Wright, Soo Jung Suh, Wendy Hayden, Nancy Comorau, helen Devinney, Heather Blain, Tyler Caroline Mills, Heather Brown, Steve Yoder, Maria Gigante, Joseph Kautzer, Adam Pellegrini, Heather Lindenman, Douglas Kern, Thomas Earles, and Nabila Hijazi. Lisa wishes to acknowledge and thank her faculty team at the Loyola University Maryland Writing Center — Craig Medvecky, Matthew Hobson, and Dominic Micer — and all of her Writing Department colleagues, most especially Peggy O'Neill. Lisa also acknowledges and fondly remembers her former colleagues at the University of Maryland University College Effective Writing Center: John Whitcraft, David Taylor, Aimee Maxfield, and Linda DiDesidero. We especially thank all the tutors who through the years have worked at the University of Maryland's Writing Center, the University of Maryland University College's online Effective Writing Center, and Loyola University Maryland's Writing Center. We have learned — and continue to learn — so much from all of you.

Leigh Ryan
University of Maryland, College Park

Lisa Zimmerelli
Loyola University Maryland

Introduction for Tutors

The Bedford Guide for Writing Tutors began in the mid-1980s as a short, somewhat basic text for tutors in a brand new training course. It aimed to help them acquire knowledge of the writing process, a vocabulary with which to discuss writing, and strategies to use as they worked with writers. Sprinkled throughout were activities, exercises, and assignments designed to help tutors practice, explore, share, and learn from one another. Almost thirty years later, this book still does all of those things. Over time, however, it has been revised to reflect growth and change in tutoring writing and in writing centers. When you finish reading and working through this book, we hope you are able to (1) appreciate the writing center as a profession, (2) understand the importance of working with both papers and writers, (3) comprehend the writing process and acknowledge the wide variety of writers who use the writing center, and (4) value the growing and changing context of writing center work.

Appreciating Writing Center Professionalism

We both begin and close *The Bedford Guide for Writing Tutors* by underscoring the professionalism associated with tutoring. As an employee, you are an extension of the writing center in which you work, and an extension of the institution that writing center serves. As a private tutor, you are providing a service to a client and forming a professional relationship. It starts with the simple behaviors you demonstrate that relate to employability—dress, manners, and the like—and extends to conduct that demonstrates a good work ethic and respect for the people and situations you encounter. We begin the book by offering you some general guidelines for your interactions with writers, other tutors, and professors in Chapter 1, "The Writing Center as a Workplace." In Chapters 8 and 9, "Research in the Writing Center" and "The Writing Center as a Community," we close the book with ways to extend that professionalism further, specifically by discussing opportunities for you to be a contributing member of a community of scholars engaged in conducting and sharing research and by introducing you to the broader writing center community beyond your individual writing center.

By permission of John L. Hart FLP and Creators Syndicate, Inc.

Working with Papers and Writers

The Bedford Guide for Writing Tutors will help you understand that you have two simultaneously important tasks whenever you sit down with a writer: to work on the paper *and* to help the writer. Think of the paper before you as a vehicle for effecting change, as a way to help the writer develop key skills and confidence. Truth is, this sounds easier than it is. Most people visit the writing center thinking something like the following:

Step 1: Visit writing center with rough draft because I want a good grade.

Step 2: Tutor tells me where and how to fix what either of us identifies as problems.

Step 3: I fix problems.

Step 4: I get a good grade.

Given the writer's expectations, it's not surprising that new tutors often respond accordingly. Seasoned tutors sometimes look back on their early experiences with writers and comment on "unlearning" or overcoming a tendency to want to fix *everything*. Indeed, we have had many conversations with tutors who have struggled with just that, tutors who knew they could not actually write the paper for a student, but nonetheless thought that only perfect papers should leave the writing center. And so they allowed sessions to extend far beyond the allotted time, or they wrote comprehensive six- to seven-page online responses to two- to three-page papers.

But if you're not producing "perfect" papers, what is your task and how do you do it? We provide strategies for what we see as your ideal task: to help writers become better writers in Chapter 2, "Inside the Tutoring Session." You can do this by reacting as a reader and demonstrating how other readers might respond, by explaining or showing possibilities and helping writers explore them, by providing examples, and by helping them identify and prioritize issues and figure out ways to deal with them. Just like learning to write, learning to tutor effectively takes time and work. The suggestions in

Chapter 2 provide you with an arsenal of tools for tutoring, tools that will give you a range of choices that allow you to consider alternatives, and try "b" or "c" if "a" doesn't seem to be connecting with the writer very well. As you get more comfortable through practice using these tools, you will learn how to use them wisely—to know when to put your pencil down and when to pick it up.

Learning about the Writing Process and the Writers You Tutor

Because writers—indeed, people—are all so different, we hope *The Bedford Guide for Writing Tutors* will help you see that there are many approaches to both the learning process and the writing process. When we don't know what to do, we typically go back to what we know, to where we are comfortable. In the process we sometimes make assumptions that everyone does things the way we do them, and we are surprised when we discover that isn't always true. Not everyone is a visual learner or begins writing an essay by donning yoga pants and brainstorming in a coffee shop. Chapter 3, "Tutoring Writers through the Writing Process," gives you a foundation so that you have an appreciation for the variety of ways writers can approach and tackle any writing task.

Building on that foundation, Chapter 4, "The Writers You Tutor," introduces you to some of the writers you will have the privilege of tutoring. *The Bedford Guide for Writing Tutors* reflects our commitment to and appreciation for the diverse writers and tutors who circulate in and out of writing centers. To that end, we have chosen to use the term *multilingual* to describe writers and tutors who are proficient in or learning two or more languages, and, in the absence of a gender-neutral pronoun, we have alternated using *she* and *he* when referring to writers and tutors. Because this book is used widely in a range of schools and countries, it is deliberately broad-based. We encourage you to explore additional strategies or considerations that fit your own tutoring situation. You may, for example, want more ideas for helping multilingual writers or students with disabilities.

Similarly, Chapter 5, "Helping Writers across the Curriculum," provides you with an understanding and overview of the most common writing assignments you may encounter in the writing center. However, depending on the institutional context of your writing center, you may want to know more about writing in the sciences or for the medical or legal professions. At the Maryland Institute College of Art (MICA), for example, students study to become professional artists and designers, and contribute to an environment conducive to the evolution of art and design. Assistance in their Writing Studio includes help with writing an artist statement (an introduction to the artist's work), as well as brief descriptions to accompany works on display in a gallery at an exhibit.

Valuing the Growing and Changing Context of Writing Center Work

Finally, *The Bedford Guide for Writing Tutors* will help you understand and value the ever-changing landscape of writing center work. For example, evolving technology has profoundly altered how we write and has influenced how we assist writers. Throughout this book we incorporate current digital practices, and we specifically highlight online tutoring and research strategies in Chapter 6, "Tutoring in the Information Age." Similarly, in Chapter 7, "Addressing Various Tutoring Situations," we give you strategies for approaching a broad range of tutoring situations while being respectful and inclusive.

Collectively, we have tutored in and directed writing centers for over fifty years. *The Bedford Guide for Writing Tutors* is a labor of love, and our hope is that it may help you become an increasingly confident and competent writing tutor. In the process, we also hope that you will come to find tutoring as exciting and rewarding as we do.

Contents

4. The Writers You Tutor   52

5. Helping Writers across the Curriculum   72

6. Tutoring in the Information Age   88

1

The Writing Center as a Workplace

Tutoring writers can be an exciting, enjoyable, and rewarding experience. You may be tutoring in a writing center, for a company, or on your own; in each case, you become part of a long history of people involved in this profession.

Being engaged in a professional activity has ethical implications for your behavior with writers; it influences how you conduct yourself as part of a group, how you relate to other tutors, and how you function as a representative of the writing center. Tutoring involves both responsibility and trust; therefore, you are encouraged to observe certain principles of conduct in your relationships with writers, other tutors, and teachers. To make apprehensive writers feel more comfortable, writing centers tend deliberately to project an inviting, relaxed atmosphere. Tutors reflect this ambience through their casual friendliness.

Occasionally, however, tutors may be tempted to behave in too casual a manner, forgetting for the moment the professional nature of tutoring. Because you may begin tutoring at the same time that you start reading this book, you should be familiar with some professional principles at the outset.

PROFESSIONALISM TOWARD THE WRITER

- When writers arrive, be pleasant and courteous. They may feel uneasy about showing their writing to a tutor, and those coming in for the first time may be unsure about writing center procedures. Make sure everyone feels welcome. Although you may intend it as a gesture of goodwill, being flippant or sarcastic may put some writers off. If you are working online with a writer, be aware of your tone. It may take a few extra moments to

1

type out a nice welcome message, but setting a friendly tone for the entire online session is important.

- Greet each writer cheerfully and indicate that you are ready to begin work, even if you are tired or under stress from school or job responsibilities. Especially in the reception area, be careful about discussing whose turn it is to tutor or making comments like, "Who wants to work with this one?" or "I guess I'll take him." Such behavior might make a writer wonder what kind of help a grudging tutor will deliver.

- It is fine to be relaxed at the writing center, but excessively informal behavior—conducting personal conversations with other tutors or casually touching students, for instance—may offend writers, especially those from certain cultural backgrounds. Similarly, when working online with a writer, be conscious of how you use digital shorthand like *LOL* or *BTW*. Such slang can be confusing and off-putting for those writers less familiar with it. However, if the writer uses digital shorthand, and it is within the guidelines of your writing center, feel free to continue in this mode, as it may make the writer more comfortable.

- Avoid negative comments about a writer's topic. The writer may have personal reasons for choosing a particular poem to explicate or something controversial to explore. Even if the writer does not seem happy about the topic, it is best to be positive from the outset to set the tone for the rest of the tutoring session.

- Honor the confidentiality of the tutoring relationship: Don't comment on or discuss writers or their papers with teachers, in front of other people, or on social media. Idle comments—whether praise or complaints—about writers may get back to them. Such comments may also be overheard by other clients who visit the writing center, making them wonder what will be said about them when they leave. If you need advice or want to vent about a difficult tutoring session, seek out your director or another administrator privately.

PROFESSIONALISM TOWARD OTHER TUTORS

- Being professional means reporting for work on time or calling and/or e-mailing beforehand if something prevents you from being there as scheduled. Like you, other tutors juggle class, work, and home schedules. Your coworkers must pick up the slack when you do not manage your time effectively.

- Be aware that carelessness or delinquency on your part makes someone else's job more difficult. Make sure that you follow all the procedures and rules of your workplace, from putting materials away to filling out tutoring reports and timesheets.

- Tutors and writers often work in close quarters, so be aware of the volume of your voice. Tidy up your workstation before you leave so that it will be ready for the next tutor.
- If you have a few idle moments, take the initiative to engage in a helpful task. Beyond tutoring, there are often odd jobs—ranging from making coffee to watering plants to reviewing surveys—that need to be done in order to keep the writing center running smoothly.

PROFESSIONALISM TOWARD TEACHERS

- Teachers need to be sure that they are evaluating a writer's own work; therefore, refrain from writing any part of a student's paper. Instead, use guiding questions and comments to help writers recognize areas for improvement and come up with their own solutions for revising their texts. Though you may sometimes recast a sentence or two as an example, be careful about how much of the writer's work you revise. If you need more examples, make up some or find exercises in a grammar handbook or online writing resource. If you find yourself tempted to revise too much of a writer's work, put your pencil down or walk away from your computer.
- As a tutor, you will hear writers' comments about instructors, assignments, and grading policies. Some comments may be negative, and some writers may press you to agree. Be careful, however, never to comment negatively to students about a teacher's methods, assignments, personality, or grading policies. Recognize that you cannot know everything that transpires in a classroom and that writers are relating their impressions or interpretations, and these may be incomplete or even inaccurate. If you cannot understand an assignment or a grading policy, suggest that the writer ask the teacher for clarification.
- Sometimes a student who is unhappy about a grade will actively seek support from a tutor for his or her dissatisfaction. Never criticize the grade that a teacher has given a paper. Just as suggesting a grade for a paper can lead to trouble, so too can acknowledging to the student that you disagree with a grade. However, you can still support the student. First, you can recognize and validate his frustration with strategies like *restatement* ("I can hear that you are really frustrated by this grade because you worked so hard on this paper"), *empathy* ("I once had a similar experience in a theology class, and I remember it took me a while to even look at the paper again for revision"), or *refocus* ("Can I help you begin to figure out what additional work remains on this paper?"). You may also prompt the

student to try to resolve grade concerns with the teacher, and then, if necessary, with other appropriate people.

- You may have had the same teacher or faced a similar situation as a student you are tutoring. Though you may commiserate, focus on helping the writer find strategies to cope rather than sharing stories. Try to support the writer and allow her to express frustrations and questions without adding your opinion. If it is appropriate, you can empower the writer by explaining the procedures in place for discussing an issue or registering a complaint.

- Some writers may ask "Is this paper good enough for a B?" and others may pressure you to suggest a grade. Assigning grades is a subjective matter that requires experience and training, and it is the teacher's job, not the tutor's. Furthermore, suggesting or insinuating a grade could create conflicts among the teacher, the student, and the writing center. Even if a paper seems well written, it is wise to be judicious with your praise. A writer may interpret your comment that "this is a good paper" to mean that it deserves an A.

As a tutor, you will help many friendly, hardworking, conscientious students become better writers. However, as in any professional setting, you may occasionally encounter some difficult situations. Whether it is the fifth paper on school uniforms you have seen, a consistently late coworker, a writer who wants you to predict a grade, or a teacher who approaches you to discuss his student's paper, we hope that these principles will help you conduct yourself in a professional manner.

To the writers you encounter, you represent the writing center. They judge the writing center not only by the competency of your tutoring but also by the attitudes, courtesy, and respect you display toward them and your coworkers.

THE MANY HATS TUTORS WEAR

Many former tutors report that their work tutoring writing prepared them well for their future professional positions. They note that paying attention to others' writing skills inevitably means honing your own, and writing well matters in any job. Important, too, however, is the development of people skills — the ability to empathize, and to adapt and respond appropriately to each individual writer's situation. Doing so means that, just like other jobs you may have had (or will have), in the writing center you will find yourself wearing many hats.

A tutor's role varies from session to session. With one writer, you ask question after question to help him figure out what he has to say about a scene in *Beowulf*. With the next, you explain the various ways of defining a

term in a definition paper. In the midst of this session, the writer vents some frustrations about being a returning student and balancing her time, so you direct her to a series of workshops for returning students. Then, a multilingual writer arrives. He is having a bit of trouble with subject and verb agreement; you pull out a piece of paper and start explaining. In your tutoring, you function variously as an ally, a coach, a commentator, a collaborator, a writing "expert," a learner, and a counselor.

The Ally

You are a friend who offers support to a writer coping with a difficult task—writing a paper. You are sympathetic, empathetic, and encouraging, and best of all, you are supportive and helpful. You explain things in terms that the writer can understand. You answer questions that may seem silly or stupid, but you take them seriously. You smile (in person or online: ☺). You understand. You commiserate. (You also have a history paper due tomorrow, and you do not expect to get much sleep tonight either!)

The Coach

In sports, coaches instruct players and direct team strategy. They do not actually do the work for the team, but rather they stand on the sidelines observing how the team functions, looking at what is going well and what needs improvement. Likewise, you stand on the sidelines. The work of writers needs to be their own, but by asking questions, making comments, and functioning as a reader, you encourage writers to think through problems and to find their own answers. You suggest ways of accomplishing tasks. You describe how to organize a comparison and contrast paper, clarify the rules for using a semicolon, or explain and help writers implement strategies for invention.

The Commentator

Sports commentators give play-by-play accounts, but they also give a picture of the whole game as it progresses. Likewise, you describe process and progress in a broader context than a writer might otherwise see. As former

Purdue University professor and writing lab director Muriel Harris explains, "The tutor-commentator provides perspective, makes connections to larger issues, gives students a sense of when and how they are moving forward."[1] You enable writers to see a paper as a whole by working with them to establish goals and by explaining what work lies ahead. You help them to acquire strategies and skills that will work not just for this paper but for others as well. You point out that making a correction in spelling or punctuation is not simply a matter of following a convention but rather of making their writing more accessible for a reader.

The Collaborator

You know that writers are supposed to do all of the work themselves, but you are discussing ideas for a paper with a particularly astute and engaged writer. She has read Kate Chopin's *The Awakening* and has focused on examining the color imagery in it. You have just read the book, so you know what she is talking about. She mentions the dinner scene, and you have an idea about the color yellow in it. Do you keep it to yourself? Probably not. More likely, the two of you discuss ideas about the imagery in a mutually engaging and even exhilarating exchange; she profits from your input and you from hers.

Such an exchange often seems like the best part of tutoring, but if you do share your ideas with writers, be wary of two potential problems. First, writers should always be responsible for and in control of their own papers. Lazy or unsure writers may try to rely on you to produce most or all of the ideas for papers—in effect, to write the paper—which should be their own work. Conversely, the overzealous tutor may usurp papers, interjecting too many ideas and leaving writers confused, no longer in control of the paper, and perhaps less confident about their writing abilities.

The Writing Expert

You may not be a writing teacher or a writing expert; nonetheless, students usually come to you assuming that you know more about writing than they do. The truth is that you probably do. Just by being a tutor, you become more knowledgeable about writing. You are an example of the adage that we learn best when we explain something to someone else.

But what do you do when you realize that you are in over your head, that you do not know how to explain a grammatical point or the options available when writing a résumé? The simple answer is to admit that you do not know and then to seek help. Check—or have the writer check—a textbook, handbook, or website; thus, you model how one can use available resources.

---

[1] Muriel Harris. "The Roles a Tutor Plays: Effective Tutoring Techniques." *English Journal* 69.9 (1980): 62–65.

You can also ask another tutor, who can often be an excellent resource. Occasionally, you may need to turn the writer over to a more knowledgeable tutor. In that case, you might sit in (or join in the chatroom if tutoring online) and learn something for the next time that you encounter a similar situation.

The Learner

This role is slightly different from the others in this list because, while it has some benefits for writers, you are the one who really gains. Writers bring papers on a wide variety of topics, some of which will be partially or entirely new to you. What, for example, causes chondromalacia, or "runner's knee," and how is it treated? How is oil extracted from shale? What does Chief Seattle say about environmental issues in his 1854 speech? What is the Ghost Dance, and how did it contribute to the massacre at Wounded Knee on the South Dakota Pine Ridge reservation? What made Robben Island, located off Cape Town, South Africa, a good location for a leper colony, an animal quarantine station, and finally, a prison? As you talk with writers, you get to enjoy learning about these and other topics. Even if you are familiar with a topic, the perspective that the writer takes may help you see it in a new or different way. For example, a student's discussion of Isabella in Shakespeare's *Measure for Measure* as a kind of "typical teenager" may lead you to consider that character differently.

Knowing little or nothing about a topic often makes you a perfect audience for a paper, so writers actually gain from your lack of expertise. Writers often have difficulty accommodating an audience; as they answer your questions and clarify their writing for you, they will learn how to adapt their texts for an audience.

The Counselor

A student's life includes much more than the writing assignment at hand, and often other issues and concerns interfere with completing the assignment. Sometimes you may find yourself playing the role of counselor, listening to writers' concerns and dealing with such issues as attitude and motivation. You may encounter a transfer student who is disgruntled because she has lost credits in changing schools, a returning student who wonders if he can continue to juggle his job and school successfully, or a graduating senior who has lost interest in school and just can't seem to get motivated. In such cases, you offer support, sympathy, and suggestions as appropriate. You refer students to workshops or programs on campus: for example, conversation groups for English language learners, time-management or study-skills seminars, résumé workshops, or GRE reviews.

You may encounter a writer whose paper is deeply personal and reveals worrisome content that makes you feel uncomfortable or ill prepared to address.

If you think a student may need professional help, speak with your director or other administrator, who will know the appropriate campus resources and can refer the student. You are not violating any privacy concerns by going to your director or administrator, and it is generally better to err on the side of caution when students reveal sentiments or ideas that make you uncomfortable.

WHEN IS A TUTOR NOT A TUTOR?

Once your friends and neighbors — or even writers you work with — realize that you are a writing tutor, they may seek your help with assignments outside the writing center. Except in special cases that only you can decide (helping a roommate or coworker, for example), it is best to restrict your tutoring to the writing center. Otherwise, you may find yourself coerced into spending your study, sleep, or family time working on someone else's paper. If you have difficulty establishing boundaries with people requesting help outside of writing center hours, talk with your director or other administrator.

EXERCISE 1A: Keeping a Personal Tutoring Journal

A journal provides a way to record your progress as a tutor, to give voice to your observations, and to write your way toward solutions to problems that you may encounter in the writing center. Your journal can be paper or online; pick the medium that feels most comfortable and natural to you. For the first several weeks of your time in the writing center, write in your journal at least once a week about your tutoring experiences. Consider including:

- Your experiences tutoring a variety of students and assignments.
- Your reflections on successful and less-than-successful tutoring sessions.
- Your observations regarding the writing process.
- Your reactions to readings, writing assignments, or topics covered in tutor meetings or other classes involving writing.

This journal may be entirely private, or it could be part of a class or writing center online forum (a blog or discussion board), where your director, other tutors-in-training, or tutors in the center are invited to read and respond. Additionally, the instructor, director, or tutors may post prompts on a regular basis (perhaps weekly) to explore issues and questions that arise as you tutor or to continue discussions about tutoring and writing begun in class or in meetings. Remember, however, that this forum must be private to maintain confidentiality and professionalism; the contents of these journals may include information that is helpful as you process various tutoring sessions, but certainly not appropriate for a public audience.

EXERCISE 1B: Participating in Public Online Discussion Forums

Public online discussion forums are a wonderful way for tutors to connect cross-institutionally. Participating in online forums will help you gain perspective on a variety of writing center practices and will provide you with the opportunity to contribute to the larger writing center community. But you don't have to contribute to participate! You should feel free to "interlope" by simply following a listserv thread or reading a blog regularly. Here are two popular options:

- E-mail listserv: Wcenter (writingcenters.org/resources/join-the-wcenter-listserv/)
- Blog: PeerCentered (www.peercentered.org/)

Additionally, many writing centers and regional writing center associations have their own social media, including blogs, and they invite contributions from anyone. See, for example, The University of Wisconsin-Madison's active blog, "Another Word," at writing.wisc.edu/blog/.

EXERCISE 1C: Investigating Your Writing Center's History

Many writing centers have existed for years, and their histories are fascinating and diverse. The following activities can help you learn more about your writing center:

- **Conduct an interview.** Find people knowledgeable about your writing center's background: the director, a previous director, the writing program director, senior faculty members, and former tutors. Consider asking the following questions:
  - When and why was the writing center established?
  - Has its mission changed over time? If so, how and why?
  - In what other ways has the writing center changed? (In the number and kinds of tutors? In services? In the number and kinds of writers served? In location? In the influences of technology?)
  - What stories can this person share about earlier days?
- **Host a panel.** Ask your director if you can pull together and facilitate a panel of people previously involved in your writing center (former directors, teachers, staff, and tutors) to address the writing center staff and talk about their experiences in the writing center. Consider recording the panel and posting it online.
- **Create an archive.** Many writing centers have boxes of "stuff" and digital files just begging to be organized and categorized: old tutoring manuals, tutor training syllabi, faculty workshop materials, writing center conference programs, etc.
- **Participate in the Peer Writing Tutor Alumni Research Project.** This project was started by three writing center directors—Harvey Kail, Paula

Gillespie, and Brad Hughes—who wanted to assess in tangible ways the impact of tutors' writing center training and experience on their lives and jobs post-graduation. Go to www.writing.wisc.edu/pwtarp/ to get started with their step-by-step guide.

- **Publish.** Share what you learn with your campus community! If your writing center or school publishes a newsletter or newspaper, consider submitting an article about your writing center's history based on your research.

EXERCISE 1D: Exploring Tutors' Roles

The roles described in this chapter are not the only ones that tutors play. Sometimes, you may find yourself functioning as parent, therapist, actor, guru, or comedian. Exploring these potential roles can be interesting and informative.

Make a list of all the roles you can imagine tutors playing, then list the strengths and weaknesses of each: What is positive or negative about each role within a tutoring session? How do these strengths and weaknesses affect tutoring? If you are working with other tutors, you might do this exercise in groups, with each group exploring the same or different roles.

2

Inside the Tutoring Session

GETTING STARTED

It is not by accident that many writing centers appear welcoming and friendly. To make writers feel more comfortable, centers are often furnished with plants, bright posters, comfortable chairs, and tables instead of desks. Writing centers often extend that friendly ambience online, with a web and social media presence that is active and helpful and offers user-friendly language and resources. Whether you meet writers in person or online, you should try to put them at ease. A casual but interested greeting and a smile — or an emoticon — can immediately make them less apprehensive about the prospect of sharing their writing. Be alert for those reluctant writers who hover about the doorway or hang out quietly in a writing center online chatroom, unsure of what to do or how to begin. Engage them with a cheerful "Can I help you?"

The following are tips to help establish rapport at the beginning of the tutoring session:

- **Introduce yourself.** Smile and ask the writer her name. Once you have settled into a comfortable place for the two of you to work, ask about the assignment and how it is going. If you have worked with the writer before, ask how the last assignment went. The exchange of pleasantries at the beginning of a session helps put the writer at ease and gets the session off to a good start. In an online environment, also ask the writer if she has had any technical difficulties or concerns that you can help resolve before you start.

- **Sit side-by-side.** Such a setup suggests that you are an ally, not an authoritarian figure who dispenses advice from behind a desk. Sitting side-by-side allows you and the writer to look at the work in progress together, but you can still position your chairs to look at each other as you converse if you like. If you do use a desk, you can have the writer sit at the side of it rather than across from you.

Just as this seating arrangement conveys a nonverbal message, be aware that your body language and clothing also express unspoken messages. Sit in a relaxed and comfortable manner, and demonstrate interest in the writer's words by leaning forward and making eye contact. Dress casually but appropriately for work. If you use a webcam when tutoring online, remember that the writer can see your facial expressions as you read his draft.

- **Give the writer control of the paper.** Keep the paper in front of the writer as much as possible. As a general rule, if you are working at a laptop or desktop computer, give the writer control of the keyboard. Positioning the writer in front of the document—whether on screen or on paper—serves to remind her (and sometimes you, the tutor!) that the writing is that of the student. Similarly, when working virtually, you can ask the writer to control the cursor (especially if you use software that enables desktop sharing).

  In both face-to-face and virtual environments, resist the urge to correct and edit mistakes as you read. Instead, indicate patterns of error, model a correction or two, and then encourage the writer to practice her own editing skills.

- **Keep resources and tools nearby.** Have scrap paper, sticky notes, highlighters, and pens and pencils handy. Also have print and online resources—like a dictionary, thesaurus, and grammar handbook—readily available. Online tutors can keep a list of resource links in a Favorites folder. Consider making other creative resources available, like a stress ball or Rubik's cube. Some writing centers keep a tactile tool or game at each tutoring station, including kinetic sand and wooden jigsaw puzzles, so that writers can do something with their hands as they talk or when they get nervous.

SETTING THE AGENDA

During the first several minutes, you and the writer will be setting at least a tentative agenda for the tutoring session, and the best way to do that is to talk or chat. Conversation not only establishes rapport but also engages the writer in the session immediately. In addition, you can learn fairly quickly about the writer, the assignment, and his approaches to and concerns about both the task at hand and about writing in general—all necessary information to determine how to spend your time together most effectively and efficiently.

As a new tutor, you may feel uncomfortable with an extended conversation. You may think that looking at the assignment description and the

Reprinted by permission of the artist, Elmar Hashimov.

writer's paper gives you something concrete to do, and you may worry that a conversation could go in unpredictable directions. Recognize, however, that this initial conversation allows you both to establish a comfortable acquaintance and to gather information and assess the writer's needs. As an intelligent, interested, and friendly audience, you will find it relatively easy to talk and learn more about the assignment and the writer. Then, you can put your newly acquired tutoring skills to work more easily and productively.

How to begin? Quite simply, ask questions and show interest.

- "What can I help you with?"
- "What assignment are you working on?"
- "Who is your audience?"
- "What are you writing about?"
- "What a fascinating topic! Why did you choose it?"
- "What approach did you take?"
- "Can you tell me (briefly) how you set up your argument?"
- "Can you tell me a little more about your writing process for this paper—how you started, how much time you gave yourself for research, and so on?"

As the writer answers, seek clarification with follow-up questions. This time devoted to conversation will reap rewards later: when you look at the paper, you will be able to match the writer's goals with what actually appears in the paper and can then more readily offer suggestions to make the writing—and the writer's approach to it—more effective.

If the assignment is unfamiliar, read through the description to be sure the writer has not forgotten or misunderstood any details. (Even if the assignment is a common one, it is probably a good idea to glance through the description in case the instructor has made any changes.) As you read the description, engage the writer with comments or questions like "I see you have to . . ." or "What did you choose for . . . ?" Asking writers to articulate the assignment—and their approach to it—often helps you uncover any misunderstandings or apprehensions that they may have.

A writer will often respond to your question "What can I help you with?" quite specifically, which simplifies setting an agenda for the session. The writer may explain, for example, that "the introduction just doesn't seem to do what I want it to" or "the paper reads too much like a list." However, be aware that some writers will simply ask for help with "proofreading," "editing," "flow," or "grammar," using these terms to cover any aspect of revising from major reorganizing to eliminating wordiness to correcting punctuation.

How you and the writer ultimately spend your time depends on the following factors:

- Where is the writer in the composing process?
- What are the constraints imposed by the assignment itself—the inherent limitations and those imposed by the teacher (such as length, number of resources to be used, and so on)?
- How much time remains before the paper is due?
- How willing is the writer to work with the tutor in order to improve the paper?
- How long is the tutoring appointment: Thirty minutes? One hour?

If you and the writer do not jointly agree on the focus of the session at the outset, then together you can determine what might be realistically accomplished in the time that you have. Managing expectations can lead to a more productive tutoring session. As you talk with the writer and look through the assignment and essay, make a list of concerns and items, either on paper or in conversation, that could be covered. Ultimately, this list should be understandable to both you and the writer. Next, prioritize the list, taking into consideration the due date. Remember that it is better to cover issues like content and organization before dealing with matters like sentence structure and grammatical errors. Perhaps you can factor in scheduling subsequent sessions if the list is long. Or the writer may prefer simply to concentrate on certain aspects this time and on others at another time.

Sometimes, a writer lacks sufficient time to truly benefit from the tutor's suggestions. There may be problems with the content or organization, for example, but the writer may only have time to correct sentence-level errors. When you encounter such a situation, explain that you cannot deal with all aspects of the paper that may need attention but will focus on the most expedient ones. Nonetheless, it is important to point out the other areas of concern, and maybe some potential resources, so that the writer is aware of them as she writes future papers.

Other times, a writer expects a tutor to review every page of a long paper, which is just not possible in a short time. In such a case, ask the writer to identify the section of the paper giving him the most difficulty. You can also explain that sentence-level problems in early pages will likely recur in later pages; you can then offer suggestions for improvement on a page or two that the writer may apply to subsequent pages.

FOUR EFFECTIVE, POWERFUL TOOLS

As a tutor, you have four powerful tools at your disposal:

- Asking questions
- Listening actively
- Facilitating by responding as a reader
- Using silence and wait time to allow a writer time to think

Used in combination, these tools can help you learn and understand better what writers' concerns or problems with writing may be. You can use them to induce writers to think more clearly and specifically about their audience, their purpose, their writing plan, or what they have already written. These tools also provide an excellent means of getting feedback to determine how well writers understand the suggestions or advice that you have given them.

Asking Questions

Questions can help you learn more about a writer's attitudes and specific problems with writing or with particular assignments. Questions fall into two broad categories—closed and open. Equally useful, closed and open questions generate different responses depending on the context.

A closed question is one like "Do you have a description of your assignment?" or "When is your paper due?" Such questions require a *yes* or *no* or a brief, limited response and yield specific information. This specific information can be very helpful. For example, the answer to a closed question like "Who is your teacher?" may tell you something about the class or assignment, especially if you have already tutored other students from that class.

An open question—like "What have you been working on in class?" or "What can I do to help?"—is broad in scope and requires more than a few words in response. Usually, an open question begins with *what, why,* or *how.* Responses to such questions, especially at the beginning of a tutoring session, can help you to determine the writer's attitude toward the task at hand. Asking "What can I help you with?" invites more response than "I see you're working on a literature review." A question like "How is the class going?" may help you to learn about the writer's performance as well as his expectations.

You can often easily and quickly modify a question from closed to open if it doesn't generate much response. For example, a simple modification of "Do you have some ideas for that section?" to "What are your ideas for that section?" asks the writer to provide those ideas instead of just saying "yes" or "no."

Listening Actively

Active listening means making a conscious effort not only to hear another person's words, but also to understand the complete message being sent. Here we examine the power of active listening through the interaction between Dwight and his tutor, Kristen. After exchanging pleasantries and settling down at a table, the two begin their session. As you follow their conversation, note Kristen's use of questions, and pay particular attention to her responses to Dwight's comments and concerns.

> *Kristen:* So, tell me what you're working on. What's your assignment, and what can I do to help?
>
> *Dwight:* I'm taking this Business Communication course and we just completed a unit on intercultural communication. For our final paper, we're supposed to explain how understanding cross-cultural differences and nonverbal language is critical to our own professional development. We have to use at least five examples in our paper.
>
> *Kristen:* That sounds like a really interesting assignment, like it would be fun to do. I haven't heard of that assignment before, so I'm a little confused. Do you have to do research for it? Tell me more.
>
> *Dwight:* No. No additional research. Not really. We are supposed to use examples from our book—there is a whole chapter on this—and from a video we watched in class. I don't know. Five to seven pages! I think it's kind of hard. I can think of cross-cultural differences from the chapter and video, but there are so many. How do I choose the best ones? I don't want to do the same ones everyone else is doing. By the time Professor Timmons looks at my paper, she might be tired of reading about handshakes and direct eye contact. And then I don't know how to put them into some kind of order. And here's the other thing: I'm kinda worried about making a stereotype. What if I end up writing something offensive?

Kristen: What I'm hearing you say is that this assignment is really frustrating you, for a whole bunch of reasons, and you just can't get started. It sounds like you're worrying about all of it at once. Let's see if we can get some kind of handle on this. Okay. You have to select at least five examples of cross-cultural differences in nonverbal communication, right?

Dwight: Yes, like the one I mentioned — how American business people expect a firm handshake and direct eye contact in introductions. But they're the obvious ones.

Kristen: Perhaps. I also heard you say that you were worried about accidentally calling up a stereotype, right? But you also told me that part of the assignment is explaining how understanding these cultural differences is important for your own professional development. Do you think you might start there, with the examples that will help you, as an American, be more aware and sensitive in intercultural exchanges? Maybe that would be an interesting place to brainstorm.

Dwight: Well, sure — there's the business greeting, how meetings are conducted, what to do at a business lunch or dinner.

Kristen: Great! And see, you've already started to organize your examples yourself. You mention the various encounters an American business person might have on a business trip and how intercultural nonverbal communication is important in each.

Dwight: You know, I was concerned because I didn't want to make stereotypes, but if I go into these differences, then I can actually explain how these differences have meaning for their cultures.

Kristen: What do you mean? Can you help me understand more?

Dwight: Like, for example, if doing business in China, it is expected that we first greet the most senior official present, and formally, too, with a title. This is a sign of respect.

Kristen: So, that has to do with the greeting. Do you have other comparative examples besides China and America?

Dwight: Sure. I know that the video had an example from Sweden — or maybe it was France? I'll review it again. And then I can move into how the business meeting is conducted. For example, my book explained that in Brazil there is a good amount of casual, small talk before getting down to serious business.

Kristen: Interesting. But remember your point that you want to provide more than just an example; you told me that you also want to provide the cultural significance behind that example.

Dwight: Oh, I can! You see, in Brazil relationship-building is really important, and so establishing a friendly, casual atmosphere at the start of a business meeting is a step toward that.

Kristen: Well it sounds to me like you have a lot to start with. And you even have a good idea of how to organize the paper.

When Dwight initially talks about his assignment, he is clearly overwhelmed and frustrated. Rather than sorting the assignment into workable tasks, he worries simultaneously about the paper's content, length, organization, and due date, and about engaging the reader. He also worries about inadvertently calling up a stereotype.

What Kristen demonstrates in this scenario is active listening, a skill that takes energy and concentration. Instead of dismissing Dwight's concerns, Kristen grants them validity with statements like "What I'm hearing you say is . . . ," "It sounds like . . . ," and "I also heard you say that . . ." She feeds back what she understands to be his message.

As the session continues, Kristen *paraphrases* Dwight's explanation of the assignment and his examples, mirroring what she heard him say earlier. This paraphrasing accomplishes two purposes: it lets Dwight know that she has heard and understood him, but it also serves as a way to check perceptions and correct any possible misunderstandings. For example, as Dwight notes, and then Kristen reminds him, it is not just the differences that are important, but the cultural meaning and significance behind those differences.

Kristen also uses questions to invite Dwight to expand on or continue his thoughts. She asks, "Do you think you might start there, with the examples that will help you, as an American, be more aware and sensitive in intercultural exchanges?" Notice that this question is closed (it can be answered by a decisive *yes* or *no* response), but it is nonetheless quite effective: Dwight immediately generates a list of categories of business relations. If Dwight had simply said "yes," then Kristen could have shifted to an open variation of the question, such as "Can you list as many examples as you can remember right now?" or "What examples were particularly interesting to you and why?" to nudge Dwight to continue his thoughts and to develop them. Kristen uses open questions when she asks, "What do you mean? Can you help me understand more?" These questions require Dwight to give very specific examples to clarify and support his claim.

Finally, Kristen uses *I* statements when she says "I'm a little confused" and "I can hear . . ." This approach places the burden of understanding on her rather than on Dwight. If she had said, "You're not explaining things clearly," Dwight might well have become defensive. Because Kristen's questions and comments are not antagonistic, Dwight is more likely to seek out and remedy the causes for her confusion rather than to justify his apprehensions.

What we can't see in this scenario is Kristen's physical engagement in the conversation—her body language. An active listener generally communicates interest and concern by posture and eye contact. Kristen is probably leaning slightly forward, with her feet on the floor, looking directly at Dwight. Her gestures of friendliness and approval, like nodding or smiling in agreement, also help to assure him that she is interested and following what he is saying. As Dwight's assignment reminds us, the cultural backdrop of your writing center will affect your interactions with writers; the important thing is to be mindful of how your nonverbal communication can further support and encourage writers.

Facilitating by Responding as a Reader

When a tutor responds as a reader, he provides the feedback and impressions he imagines the writer's audience might have. He does not presume to know all of the answers, but rather poses questions and offers feedback that help bridge the gap between the writer and her audience. Take, for example, the following situation. Jane initiates a chat with her online tutor, Javier. Jane has written the first draft of a paper for an *Introduction to Poetry* class and she pastes the first two paragraphs into the chat window:

◯ Chat Example: Responding as a Reader

Jane entered the room.
Javier entered the room.

Javier says: Hi! What can I help you with?
Jane says: Here is my paper so far. What do you think?

Emily Dickinson, her poetry, and her style of writing all reflect her own feelings as well as her own ultimate dreams. Her withdrawal from the world and her impassioned art were also inspired in part I think by a tragic romance. A series of tormented and often frankly erotic letters were found to prove that this unsuccessful romance had a strong impact on her emotions — enough impact to seclude her from any outside life. This paper concerns two of Emily Dickinson's poems, number 288 and number 384, which are both prime examples that reflect the dejection she was experiencing.

In poem number 288, Dickinson reveals her loneliness. In line number one, she introduces herself as "Nobody," as if it is her plural name. Nobody also refers to someone that people do not know much about. I think the word Nobody uses both meanings in this poem. She then asks the reader if he or she is Nobody too.

Jane's paragraphs probably raise many questions for Javier. Looking at only the first sentence, for example, he might wonder: "What feelings are reflected? What dreams? How does Dickinson's style reflect these?" But such questions only mirror the confusion that Jane is experiencing at this stage in her writing. Though it is clear that she has thought about some ideas, she remains unfocused. She needs help with sorting through, clarifying, and articulating those ideas. Javier can assist by reacting as a reader, requesting more information and clarification, helping the writer develop critical awareness, and refocusing and prompting the writer.

REACTING AS A READER. One way a tutor can assist a writer is to react as a reader as they go through the text. Typically, responding as a reader means one of them reads aloud, then as the tutor reacts to what has been written, the writer can observe or listen. Where does the tutor smile with pleasure or understanding? Nod in agreement or appreciation? Wrinkle his brow in confusion or frustration? Not only can he show the writer where she connects well with her audience, but he can use his responses to reflect or indicate places where a lack of clarity perplexes or distracts him, and elicit more information about the writer's intended meaning. Then, instead of making judgments about the draft with statements like "This list isn't clear," he can describe his reactions using "I" statements, and ask questions that invite the writer to further examine, explore, and clarify her ideas and approaches. He might, for example, say "I'm not sure what you mean by listing A, B, and C in that order. Did you do that for a specific reason?"

◯ Chat Example: Reacting as a Reader

Javier says: In your introduction, you say that Dickinson's poetry reflects her feelings and dreams and her dejection about the unhappy romance that inspired it. But when I finish that paragraph, I'm a bit confused. I'm not sure exactly what your paper is going to be about. Can you briefly explain what the overall purpose of your paper is in here?

Jane says: Ok. Well, basically, I wanted to make the case that 'tragic romance' is a kind of major theme for the poems I chose.

Jane's introduction mentions several aspects of Dickinson's poetry, and it is unclear to Javier which one(s) her paper will focus on. *I* statements allow Javier, the tutor, to show Jane his experience and confusion as a reader, and invite her to resolve it. She will perhaps struggle to articulate her intended focus and may come to some new realizations about that focus that clarify it for both herself and her audience.

Javier used comments that simply and honestly conveyed his response to Jane's paper as he (or she) read it. Some writing centers use the term *practice audience* to describe the tutor's role as he reacts as a reader, a phrase that may help to clarify that role for the writer. This term gives the tutor authority to respond as he models the potential reactions of a future audience, one who will not have the writer nearby to answer questions or offer explanations, and it also makes him appear less judgmental.

REQUESTING INFORMATION. Questions such as "Can you tell me more about . . . ?" can help writers to clarify their thinking, consider the whole paper or an aspect of it more critically, refocus their thoughts, or continue a line of thinking further.

○ Chat Example: Requesting Information

Javier says: Why did you choose these two poems? Can you tell me more about them?

Jane says: They were the ones we covered in class. But there were two others that were in the book that I thought might work. Do you think I should include those, too?

Of the many poems written by Emily Dickinson, Jane chose only two to discuss. Javier's question gives Jane an opportunity to articulate and examine the reasons for her choice. In this case, the reason was simply that she was limiting her choice to poems covered in class. Including the other poems may help Jane understand more clearly the claims she wants to make in her paper.

REQUESTING CLARIFICATION. When writers' answers or writing is vague, encourage them to clarify points by asking, "What is your idea here?", "What are you thinking?", "What do you want to say?", "What do you want your reader to know in this paragraph?", "How does this idea connect with what you said before?", "What do you mean by . . . ?", or "Tell me more about. . . ." To be sure you are following and understanding what a writer intends, restate the content of the message: "What I'm hearing you say is . . . Do I have it right?"

○ Chat Example: Requesting Clarification

Javier says: You say Dickinson's poetry reflects her feelings. What do you mean by 'feelings'? Which feelings?

Jane says: I thought it was obvious? I talk about loneliness in the first paragraph.

Javier says: Yes, I see that. Is that the only "feeling" you will be discussing? Are there others?

Jane's reference to feelings in the introduction is vague, so Javier's questions lead Jane to consider her intentions more carefully and come to a clearer understanding of what she means to say. As she responds, he could encourage her to relate her answers to the poems by asking, "How are Dickinson's feelings reflected in the poems you chose?"

DEVELOPING CRITICAL AWARENESS. Writers sometimes plan or write whole papers without adequately evaluating audience or purpose, and one of the best questions that you can pose is "So what?" That question, or versions of it—such as "Why does anyone [your audience] want or need to know about that?"—encourages writers to think about their purpose in addressing their audience. "So what?" also makes them consider and justify other points in the paper, as do questions like "Why would that be so?" and "Can you give me an example of . . . ?"

> ### ◯ Chat Example: Developing Critical Awareness
>
> **Javier says:** You indicate that the word *Nobody* is important in this poem. Why would that be so?
>
> **Jane says:** Well, it's connected to the feeling of loneliness. Actually, now that I think about it, I think it's tied to sadness, too.

Javier asks this question because Jane has singled out the word *Nobody* as being significant, but she does not clearly explain why. His question encourages Jane to justify its importance and relate it more concretely to the poems.

REFOCUSING. To get writers to refocus or rethink their writing, it is useful to get them to relate their approach to another idea or approach, using questions like "How would someone who disagrees respond to your argument?" "How is that related to . . . ?" or "If that's so, what would happen if . . . ?"

> ### ◯ Chat Example: Refocusing
>
> **Javier says:** You mentioned Dickinson's "withdrawal from the world." Didn't Dickinson also have a phobia, a fear of public places? How might that relate to her "withdrawal from the world"?
>
> **Jane says:** That's right! We talked about that in class. That definitely seems related to her theme of loneliness. . . .

Because Javier knows something about Jane's topic—Dickinson's phobia—he contributes an aspect that she could at least bear in mind as she re-evaluates. His question does not demand that Jane address this aspect in her paper; it merely alerts her to a dimension she forgot to include and asks her to examine whether she should consider it.

PROMPTING. To get writers to continue or follow their line of thinking further, encourage them with questions like "What happens after that?" or "If that is so, then what happens?"

◯ Chat Example: Prompting

Javier says: What words or phrases suggest to you that she was lonely? How do those words or phrases show loneliness?

Jane says: Oh, I underlined a bunch of lines. They don't all mention the word "lonely," but they seem to imply it.

Javier says: Can you show me a few, so we can discuss how they relate to your paper?

Javier's questions encourage Jane to pursue her line of thinking about loneliness and references to loneliness within the poems.

As a facilitator, you function as a sounding board or mirror, reflecting back to writers what you hear them trying to communicate. Your primary purpose is to evoke and promote writers' ideas. As you become increasingly comfortable with tutoring and better able to size up the writers with whom you work, you may feel more at ease with occasionally offering opinions about or suggestions for content. But beware: The paper must remain the responsibility of the writer.

Using Silence and Wait Time

Try this experiment: Get a watch or clock with a second hand. At the start of a minute, turn around or place the clock out of sight. When you think that a minute has elapsed, look back. How close did you come? Thirty seconds? Forty-five? Chances are you stopped a little too soon, and that is what we tend to do when we try to make ourselves wait: We jump in a little too soon.

As a tutor, you should learn when and how to pause and be silent in a tutoring session. Occasionally, writers need time to digest what has been discussed or to formulate a question. They also need time to think about a response when you pose a question. Often, tutors are tempted to quickly rephrase a question or even answer it themselves when a writer does not respond after a moment or two. If you feel this temptation, try waiting a little longer than you think you should; then wait some more. This deliberate use of wait time communicates to writers that they are expected to think and arrive at answers on their own. You might even create an excuse to get up and leave for a few minutes; go to the restroom or get a drink of water. When working online with writers, silence is sometimes even more difficult to bear, as the blinking cursor seems to demand an immediate response. Feel free to type "take your time" or "I have to leave the computer for a couple of minutes; I'll be right back!" to give the writer some online breathing room.

Thinking time is especially important when a new aspect of a topic arises, and writers may even need a few moments on their own to do some writing. Try initiating short breaks that allow writers five or even ten minutes to freewrite, brainstorm, draft, or revise a section of a paper, or to complete an activity that relates to what you have just been discussing. When they finish, you can review their work with them. When chatting online, simply give writers a set amount of time to work on a discrete task: "I'm going to give you five minutes; I'll be here when you want to resume." Resist the urge to maintain constant online chatter; instead, give them the time and space necessary to compose their thoughts.

USING A HANDBOOK

A handbook serves as a concise and ready reference or manual on a particular subject. The late Diana Hacker described *The Bedford Handbook* as "small enough to hold in your hand . . . [and able to] answer most of the questions you are likely to ask as you plan, draft, and revise a piece of writing."[1] Whether seeking general help on new ways to think about narrowing a topic or more specific advice on a grammatical point or documentation, even the best writers frequently consult a handbook; no one knows all the answers by heart. As you work with writers, do not hesitate to consult a handbook and suggest that they bring their own handbooks to future tutoring sessions. Together, you can mark sections that writers may want to reference again as they continue to revise. Not only can you help them answer their questions accurately, but you will also be modeling the behavior of good writers.

WRAPPING UP A SESSION

Some sessions end gracefully when you and the writer finish addressing the writer's concerns and needs; however, not all sessions are ready to end when

---

[1]Diana Hacker and Nancy Sommers. *The Bedford Handbook*, 9th ed. Boston: Bedford/ St. Martin's, 2014.

the allotted time is almost up. There may even be awkwardness: Another writer may be waiting for you, or you may be anxious to pack up and run to class. One good way to handle wrapping up a session is to watch the clock unobtrusively and announce when there are five to ten minutes left. After finishing up what you are working on, you can ask the writer if there is anything specific that he wants to cover in those last minutes or if he has any remaining questions you can answer before he leaves. In some writing centers, tutors complete a report form summing up what was accomplished; inviting the writer to contribute or comment on the form can also serve as a graceful way to wrap up a session. Online tutors often provide a final checklist; the tutor can ask the writer to help generate the list.

All of these ideas may also help you and the writer plan her next steps for revision. This planning is a critical step in the writing process, as writers often feel at a loss—even just a few hours after they've met with you—when they are once again alone with their papers. In addition to asking the writer to summarize what was accomplished in the session, you can ask her to articulate what specific writing tasks she still needs to complete. She may need help prioritizing and sorting these tasks. Should she go through and correct the comma splices first? Or should she revise her thesis and send the revision to her professor to review?

Just as you greet the writer with a smile, close similarly by congratulating him on his progress and by wishing him the best of luck as he continues his work. One positive way to close the session is to set up the next appointment in the writing center, either with you or another tutor!

EXERCISE 2A: Observing Tutors' and Writers' Body Language

View a video of a tutoring session with the sound off. Alternatively, watch ten minutes of a situation comedy, drama, or interview on television, again with no sound. Observe the body language and facial expressions of the tutor and writer or the TV characters. What messages are communicated? How?

EXERCISE 2B: Observing Tutoring Sessions

Observe several experienced tutors in sessions as they work with writers. (Be sure to first get permission to sit in from both tutor and writer.) Notice how tutors greet writers and establish rapport. Pay attention to the ways in which tutors learn what writers want help with and decide what to work on. How does the tutor engage the writer, phrase questions, and respond to the writer's concerns? What does body language convey about tutors and writers? How is a session ended?

If you are an online tutor, read chat sessions or advice from experienced tutors. How do they use questions in their advice? How is tone conveyed in an online medium? How do they explain difficult concepts? What kinds of examples do they use?

When each session ends, talk with the tutor. Ask specific questions about how and why the tutor conducted the session as he or she did. You may want to complete a form like the one below for each session you observe.

TUTOR OBSERVATION SHEET

Your name: _____

Tutor's name: _____

Date: _____ Length of session: _____

Class the student's paper is for, or other reason for coming to the center:
_____
_____

Description of the assignment: _____

Areas covered in the session:

What helped the student or worked in the session?

What was tried but didn't help the student or didn't work?

Comments and reflections on the session:

Final thoughts:

EXERCISE 2C: Working with Handbooks and Other References

When you are tutoring, questions will come up that you cannot answer on your own. You may be uncertain about the parts of a proposal, a rule for using semicolons, or documentation according to the American Psychological Association (APA) format. In these cases, you may have to check references as you help writers. Such resources vary from writing center to writing center, but most centers have a collection of writing guides and handbooks, a list of helpful online resources, and handouts with explanations and exercises.

To familiarize yourself with the resources available at your writing center, explore them and note at least two places — one text-based and one online — where you could find the following information:

1. Accepted formats for business letters
2. An explanation and exercise on subject-verb agreement
3. Discussion of thesis statement, with examples
4. Strategies for tightening wordy sentences
5. Guidelines for evaluating a website
6. Rules for when to spell out numbers or use figures
7. Exercises for correcting comma splices
8. Advice on writing and formatting résumés
9. A discussion of subordination for emphasis
10. An explanation of cause and effect as a pattern of development
11. Guidelines for putting together a PowerPoint presentation
12. The format for documenting a selection in an anthology using the Modern Language Association (MLA) style
13. The rules for use of *who* and *whom*
14. Ways to avoid using sexist language
15. A list of common spelling errors
16. An explanation of passive and active voice
17. The conventions for referring to authors in the text of a literary paper
18. A list of logical fallacies with explanations and examples
19. Guidelines for creating an entry in an annotated bibliography
20. Information on what to consider with scannable résumés
21. Explanations and examples of paraphrasing effectively
22. The correct spelling for the past tenses of *cancel* and *travel*
23. Information on e-mail etiquette ("netiquette")
24. Rules for subject-verb agreement with collective nouns like *committee*, *audience*, and *couple*
25. Rules for using abbreviations with proper names

EXERCISE 2D: Role-playing the Tutoring Session

Role-playing activities will help you to practice the tutoring techniques that are discussed in this chapter. If you are not using this book in conjunction with a class or training program, try to gather a group of tutors from your writing center who are willing to participate. Various role-playing scenarios are listed in Appendix C.

3

Tutoring Writers through the Writing Process

How does your day begin at the writing center? Do you exchange greetings with other tutors, pour yourself a cup of coffee, and check your schedule? Do you unlock the door to your one-room office and post a sign-up sheet on the door? Or do you settle in at your desk, open up your laptop, and begin a chat session? Writing centers differ widely in their facilities, procedures, and resources; however, you will find one constant from center to center: writers seeking help as they work through different stages of the writing process. Let us meet a few:

- As he takes a seat, Tom waves several sheets of paper. "Here are my notes," he tells the tutor. "I did a collecting project in my folklore class, and now I have to write a paper about what I learned. I have a bunch of ideas, but I'm not sure which ones would be good to use."

- Keisha initiates an online chat session to get help on her lab report. She types, "This is the first lab report of the semester. It's for my biology class, and I've never written one before. Am I off to a good start? I don't really understand what to do."

- Rummaging through her bag, Maria pulls out a draft of an essay for a graduate school application. She describes it as "boring" and asks, "What can I do to make it more interesting for the people who read these essays?"

- Chu opens her laptop and pulls up her paper: summaries of several articles on the role of psychology in education. "I just want to make sure my paper is right," she explains. As she fishes a piece of paper out of her notebook, she adds, "We got this handout explaining summaries, and it's got a list of mistakes you can make in summaries. I know I didn't plagiarize, but I'm not sure about some of the others."

- Miguel shares his paper online at the start of a video chat session. He explains, "I did this paper for my business writing class. I think the paper's okay, but I always have trouble with things like commas and semicolons. Please edit my punctuation."

Each of these writers is at a different stage in the writing process. Before we look at the specific stages, let us take a broader look at the writing process. The work of composition researchers and theorists like Janet Emig, Sondra Perl, Linda Flower, Peter Elbow, and Donald Murray shows that the linear model of prewriting, writing, and revising is inadequate. We now recognize that writing is a process of discovery—of exploring, testing, and refining ideas, then figuring out the most effective way to communicate those ideas to an audience. As Peter Elbow explains, "Meaning is not what you start out with but what you end up with."[1] Writing is also recursive, which means that as writers we continually return to earlier portions of a draft, generating new ideas and deleting others, writing and rewriting in order to move forward with the paper. Some writers make global revisions—major changes in content, focus, organization, point of view, or tone—after completing a first draft. Others follow the example of a student writer who recently explained, "As soon as I start writing even just a few words, I start revising." Throughout this backward and forward movement, we struggle to conform to the constraints of academic and disciplinary writing conventions. Simultaneously, we go about the complicated tasks of creating meaning while we negotiate the needs of the reader with our goals as the writer. Look at the following list of writing experiences to see if you can identify with any of them. Have you ever

- written and rewritten for hours, only to find that you have two useful sentences from many pages?
- written a section midway through your paper that forced you to make significant changes in what you had written in previous pages?
- carefully made a list of the important points to include in a paper and then discovered partway through writing that two of the points were unnecessary?
- struggled to fit a sentence at the end of a paragraph and then discovered that it fit perfectly at the beginning?
- spent an evening writing and rewriting an introduction, unable to get it together, and then had the perfect introduction spring forth when you began writing the next day?
- returned again and again to your thesis, changing it little by little as you worked out the argument in your essay?
- tried to write an e-mail and found that you had to write the angry, "no-holds-barred" e-mail before you could write the more controlled, reasonable one?

---

[1]Peter Elbow. *Writing without Teachers.* New York: Oxford University Press, 1998, 15.

Shoe-New Business: © 1990 Jim MacNelly. Distributed by King Features Syndicate, Inc.

As you can see, we cannot outline the writing process as we can a recipe in a cookbook. No single set of simple steps is guaranteed to produce an effective paper every time. As William Zinsser notes, "Writing is no respecter of blueprints—it's too subjective a process, too full of surprises."[2] Nonetheless, writing teachers and books on writing offer a variety of helpful descriptions of the process. These descriptions enable us to think of writing as something that happens in stages and to talk about it more easily with other writers. Most importantly, at each stage we can discuss a variety of workable strategies with the writers seeking our help, strategies that fit with our goal as writing tutors: *to make the people we work with more effective writers by facilitating changes in the way in which they view and produce writing.*

Tom, Keisha, Maria, Chu, and Miguel are all working their way through the writing process, sorting through ideas, getting them down on paper, and fine-tuning their presentation. In this chapter, we offer a general guide to the stages of the writing process—prewriting, drafting, and revising—and provide some specific guidelines and strategies for working with writers at each stage in the writing process. Each section includes a brief discussion about one of the writers introduced at the beginning of this chapter, how his or her writing concerns fit into that particular stage, and how a tutor can help writers throughout the writing process.

Like the writing process, tutoring is dynamic. The interaction between tutor and writer—as questions, answers, and ideas flow back and forth—largely determines the content and direction of any tutoring session. What works with one writer, however, may not be as successful with another; therefore, you need to be ready with a variety of approaches and to be flexible about using them. As you become more proficient at tutoring, you will develop your own style and be able to add your own suggestions to those given here.

---

[2]William Zinsser. *On Writing Well: An Informal Guide to Writing Nonfiction.* 6th ed. New York: HarperCollins, 2006, 63.

Stages of the Writing Process

PREWRITING

Focusing on thoughts and ideas

Considering audience

Organizing loosely

Creating a workable plan

DRAFTING

Creating an initial draft

REVISING AND EDITING (USUALLY IN MULTIPLE DRAFTS)

Global Revision: Improving content, organization, tone

Sentence-level Revision: Strengthening and clarifying

Editing: Correcting errors in grammar, punctuation, and mechanics

Proofreading: Looking for typographical errors, omitted words, and other
mistakes

PREWRITING

The prewriting stage consists of invention and planning. To generate ideas,
we may use such strategies as freewriting, brainstorming, researching, or
observing. Then, we plan our writing, focusing our thoughts and ideas and
deciding how we should organize them. As an important part of prewriting,
we also consider the audience we are addressing and our purpose for addressing them. Asking ourselves "To whom am I writing?" (the audience) and
"Why?" (the purpose) helps us to determine what information to include and
how to present it. We can then organize our ideas, at least loosely, into some
workable plan.

Both Tom and Keisha are at the prewriting stage. Tom is unsure of what
to do with the notes from his folklore project. First, he needs to identify and
assess his audience and his purpose. Then, he needs to see how the information that he has gathered fits with that purpose. Does he have enough information to at least start a draft? How can he effectively arrange his material?
Keisha seems confused about how to begin her lab report and is overwhelmed
by the idea of producing the first assignment for the course. To get started,
Keisha could explore writing conventions related to science, particularly what
is expected in a lab report. If she understands the genre of the lab report better—especially its audience, purpose, and format—she will feel more confident about organizing the findings from her research and experiments.

For writers like Tom and Keisha, who are just getting started on an assignment, it can be tremendously helpful—and relieving—to consider the writing process as a series of smaller, manageable tasks rather than one huge, seemingly impossible undertaking.

Tutors can help writers discover what it is they want to say by using a variety of techniques. Brainstorming (listing), freewriting, and clustering (branching) are discussed here, but you may want to check writing handbooks and textbooks to learn about other techniques.

Brainstorming (Listing)

Brainstorming involves focusing on a topic and tossing out, thinking through, and refining ideas to find ways to approach it. As writers list and play with ideas on a specific topic, you can ask questions to prod and encourage them to extend their ideas further.

For example, tutor-in-training Andrea comes into the writing center for help in getting started on the "How I Write" assignment in Exercise 3D of this chapter. Her tutor suggests that Andrea brainstorm a list of anything and everything that comes to mind when she thinks about how she completes a writing assignment. As she reads the list, the tutor asks questions to prompt Andrea to think and generate more ideas. The following is Andrea's list with the tutor's prompting questions:

Andrea's Brainstorming List	Tutor's Follow-up Prompting Questions
✓ wear comfortable clothes	Such as? Why?
✓ get my desk completely clear	Why?
✓ keep rereading the assignment description	When? To get started? As you write? Why? How does reading it over and over help you?

✓ PROCRASTINATE	Why did you put this word in caps? How do you procrastinate? What do you do? Why do you procrastinate?
✓ write out some ideas on paper, put them on my computer, and move them around	What do you mean by "move them around"? What do you do after that? Do you work only on the computer after that?
✓ call my dad and read the paper to him	Why? How does that help?
✓ write — rewrite — rewrite — rewrite	What do you mean by "write"? Why did you write "rewrite" three times?
✓ make sure I have a strong (funny if possible) introduction	Why? How do you do that? When do you write the intro?
✓ put my hair in a ponytail	Why? How does this relate to wearing "comfortable clothes"?
✓ try not to use a form of "to be" in the first sentence	Why? How does this relate to having "a strong introduction"?
✓ recall Ms. Coakley — my English teacher sophomore year	How did she affect your writing? What did you learn from her that affects your writing today?

As writers' ideas evolve, you can paraphrase or mirror what you hear writers saying in order to clarify, check, and sum up lines of thought. Pose questions that guide them toward considering the audience, such as "What does your audience know about . . . ?" or "How can you make that clear to your audience?" You might also play devil's advocate and suggest an opposing viewpoint to writers. Responding to you will force them to examine their own ideas more thoroughly.

Freewriting

Ask writers to put pen to paper (or fingers to keyboard) and simply let ideas on the topic flow for ten minutes. Tell them to write words, phrases, sentences, or questions but to ignore punctuation and spelling. If they get stuck, you can tell them to rewrite the last few words over and over until the ideas begin to flow again. Freewriting at the computer can be a quick and convenient way to get started. Allow the writer time to type in a list of ideas or thoughts on a topic. As you and the writer talk about the list and relationships among ideas emerge, these thoughts can be rearranged on the screen using cut-and-paste commands.

Take, for example, Zachary, who comes into the writing center for help with a research paper for an "Anthropology of Magic" class. There is no prompt; he simply has to pick a topic. Zachary has selected tarot cards. His tutor sits him down at a computer, asks him to freewrite, and leaves him for five minutes. Zach comes up with the following paragraph.

> *What do I know about tarot cards? You can tell your fortune with them. How accurate are they? I had this lady read mine at the Renaissance Festival last month. She was pretty accurate. I'm not sure how many cards there are. How do you learn to read them? Did anyone ever do any scientific investigation of them? Results? Where did they come from/start? Tarot cards. Tarot cards. The word "tarot" sounds unusual, maybe foreign. Do people all over the world use them? Sometimes in crossword puzzles — the word. What's on the cards? Pictures. Of what?*

Zach and his tutor review together what Zach has written, looking for key words, phrases, or questions that seem promising. They focus on those and discuss or brainstorm. Zach's paragraph offers a wealth of details to explore further. The tutor might ask questions that will help Zach uncover more possibilities in key words and phrases like "accurate," "learn to read them," "foreign [word]," and "scientific investigation." Zach's reference to having tarot cards read at the Renaissance Festival might lead to questions about where others go to have tarot cards read.

Clustering (Branching or Webbing)

Clustering not only helps writers explore their subject but also suggests how they might organize their ideas. With the writer, make a diagram with the central topic in the middle. Then, as you talk or chat with the writer about aspects of the topic, ask how each relates to the central topic and draw branches that show the relationships. Effective with pen and paper, clustering also works especially well at the computer and in online synchronous forums with drawing capabilities. In fact, using drawing tools, color, and highlight functions can help make these exercises more vivid for the writer.

The diagram on the following page shows how one writer explored the topic of wetlands with a tutor. They began with the central topic—wetlands— in the middle. As they discussed aspects of the topic, the tutor asked questions about why and how each aspect related to the central topic. Eventually, the writer ended up with four issues related to wetlands: parts, wildlife, importance, and legislation—each of which had several sub-issues.

Other Suggestions for Prewriting

With most writers, asking probing questions and discussing the answers can be enough to help them explore and generate ideas about a topic. For those who find coming up with ideas more difficult, a different perspective or way

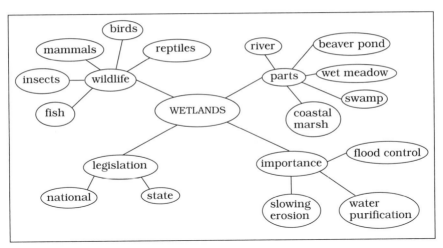

Clustering Diagram

of looking at a topic can be useful. Asking writers to engage in one of the following exercises will not generate a paper, but, at the least, it will offer some avenues to investigate.

- Imagine a scene that relates to the topic, and describe it. Try the same thing with a sound or smell.
- Imagine yourself as someone else—your older brother, your mother, your boss. How would that person look at the topic? What would he or she say about it?
- Write about the topic in an e-mail to someone with whom you feel comfortable.
- If you could write this paper without constraints, what would you write about, and how would you go about it?

DRAFTING

In the drafting stage, we get our ideas down on paper in an initial draft. Many people assume that they must write their first drafts alone—in their rooms, at the library, or in a corner of a coffee shop. While this may work for some, other writers might find it helpful to draft a portion of a paper, like the introduction, in the writing center where they can get some immediate feedback.

Consider again Tom's folklore paper. If his ideas for the paper are adequate, he might rough out an organizational strategy and begin drafting the introduction during the tutoring session, discussing his plans and thoughts at appropriate points. Similarly, while online with her tutor, Keisha might pull up a lab report template and begin working on one or two sections.

Once writers have generated sufficient ideas to get started, you can help them to organize those ideas and plan to write. A note of caution: Some writers want to begin organizing a paper when they have only a few sketchy ideas, but continuing down this trail usually leads to a weak paper. You can help writers avoid this pitfall by making sure that they have clearly identified their audience, their goal or purpose in relation to that audience, and what they hope to accomplish in the paper. If the writer has his assignment description, review the purpose and scope of the assignment, as well as the instructor's expectations. You can help writers organize and plan in several ways:

- Ask if they know the conventions of and formats for the kind of paper that they are working on. What does a cover letter accompanying a résumé typically include? What are the options for organizing a comparison-and-contrast paper or a literature review? What should be included in a lab report? If writers are unsure, explain. If you also are unsure, check a handbook or guide to writing.

- Help writers explore options by mapping out how the paper might be organized. Rather than make a formal outline, which can be too rigid and confining for many writers, suggest that the writer generate a more informal diagram, such as a list or flowchart similar to the one below. Writers can easily see the general shape of the paper but will feel more open to shuffling parts around if necessary.

INFORMAL OUTLINE

DEFINITION

tachycardia (rapid heartbeat)

CAUSES

exercise

being frightened

medication

overactive thyroid

alcohol (and drug) withdrawal

DIAGNOSIS

electrocardiogram (ECG)

electrophysiologic study (EPS)

TREATMENT

electric current

medication

- Ask the writer to start drafting the thesis and topic sentences. It might be helpful to see the main ideas worked out in full sentences. These sentences can be a jumping-off point when the writer goes to compose on his own. Be sure to let the writer know that these sentences may be revised as he continues working on the paper.

REVISING

Revision consists of two stages: *global revision*—in which we improve the "big picture" of our papers by looking at issues like content, organization, and tone—and *sentence-level revision*—in which we attend to the finer points of our writing by strengthening and clarifying sentences and correcting errors in grammar, punctuation, and mechanics.

Global Revision

Global revisions refer to the paper's overall development and organization. When making global revisions, we think big and consider whether the paper addresses the topic in a meaningful and logical way. We ask questions like "Will my audience be able to follow and understand what I've written?" "How do I come across to my audience?" "Have I included enough information?" In answering these questions, we often realize that major changes in content, focus, organization, point of view, and tone are necessary. Some writers resist this stage, bringing their first draft of a paper to the writing center with the belief that it is their last.

Maria, the graduate school applicant, needs help making global revisions. She has a draft but wants to make it more interesting to the reader. To do that,

© 2015 Zits Partnership. Distributed by King Features Syndicate, Inc.

she needs to first identify her audience and purpose for writing. Who will be reading her essay? Why is she writing to them, and what will they be looking for? She can then consider what kinds of changes to make in her essay and perhaps rearrange, add, or delete sections in order to make her writing more effective.

With her summary of articles on the role of psychology in education, Chu is most likely at the revising stage as well. Her teacher's list, "Properties of a Poorly Written Summary," warns against being verbose, offering inadequate or incomplete information, plagiarizing, adding useless material, and being too subjective. As she and the tutor read through her paper, they will be able to determine what she may need to revise.

Start by asking questions and talking with the writer about the paper's audience, topic, content, and structure so that you can give the writer the opportunity to indicate troublesome areas. As you then read through the paper together, you can compare what the writer has told you with what is actually on the page.

As writers talk about their ideas or read aloud, ask questions or make comments in order to help them clarify their thinking and offer suggestions for improvement. Be an active listener, and reflect what you hear after the writer has spoken. For example, you might respond with a statement like "What I'm hearing you say is that your audience is composed of other computer science majors, and you're trying to convince them that. . . ." At this stage, focus on the larger issues of *development* and *organization*. Not only are they more important than matters of style or mechanics, but you might also end up spending much of the tutoring session on a section that is ultimately deleted.

DEVELOPMENT

- Did the writer follow through on points raised in the thesis?
- Did the writer offer enough supporting details and examples?
- Did the writer explain relationships between ideas?

ORGANIZATION

- Did the writer organize according to a particular scheme or format?
- Did the writer organize in a logical manner?
- Did the writer organize according to the needs of a specific audience?

If you are tutoring online, you may not be able to communicate immediately with the writer; however, that should not prevent you from asking questions. Let the writer know your reaction as a reader. Consider framing your comment in the following way: "I think you're trying to refer back to the thesis here, but I'm not sure. Can you make that connection more explicit?"

The first statement will alert the reader to the global problem; the question will provide a starting place as the writer attempts to address the problem.

As you go through the paper together, you may be able to identify places where the argument is unsubstantiated, where the writer may need to conduct further research in order to find and incorporate more compelling sources. If you see an idea that is lacking support, consider logging on to the library's home page and helping the writer conduct a database search. (For more about online research, see Chapter 6.)

OTHER SUGGESTIONS FOR GLOBAL REVISION

- Consider reading the paper aloud. Asking writers to read aloud engages them more in the tutoring session; however, explain that you will interrupt whenever you have a question or comment. Occasionally, you may prefer to read—reacting and commenting as you go. In any case, do not simply let writers sit there and watch you read silently, for that will only increase any discomfort that they may be feeling.

- Read the paper as a naive reader, and indicate those places where it needs more details or more specific evidence. For example, if you read a sentence like "Watching the university's production of *Hamlet* was an exciting experience," ask what the writer means by "exciting." What exactly was it about this production that made it exciting? If you read something such as "My grandfather was a kind and generous person," ask for some specific examples or anecdotes that demonstrate his kindness and generosity.

- Stop at the end of a paragraph or section of the paper to summarize what you have just read and to explain what you anticipate will follow. If what you say does not match the writer's intended message, she can see where misinformation, extraneous details, or other cues misdirect the reader.

- Don't overwhelm the writer with too many suggestions for improvement at one time. First, see if you can identify the major recurring issues that impede the readability of the paper. Then, try to find one or two sections or sentences that represent these issues, and spend some time working with the writer on these smaller pieces of the paper. If the writer seems frustrated, it may be better to select problems that are fairly easy to deal with in order to give him or her a more successful tutoring session. You can indicate that other areas need work and suggest that the writer make another appointment to attend to them.

Sentence-level Revision

When making sentence-level revisions, we try to improve individual sentences by cutting excessive words, clarifying confusing or improperly constructed sentences, or trying to find more exact words for the ideas that we want to express. In the editing stage, we correct errors in grammar, punctuation, and mechanics.

Sentence-level revisions involve strengthening and varying sentences as well as refining style. Inappropriate or imprecise language, wordiness, and choppiness are common problems in student papers. To help writers recognize these problems and learn to correct them, concentrate on a small section—a paragraph or several sentences. Later, writers can apply what they have learned to the rest of the paper. This approach also reminds writers that they are ultimately responsible for revising their papers.

Online tutors should be careful not only to identify mistakes but also to explain how writers can identify and correct future sentence-level errors. Although the reviewing function in word-processing programs can be helpful, avoid editing the paper. Rather, copy and paste a problematic sentence or two into your comments, identify the mistake(s), and provide feedback.

OTHER SUGGESTIONS FOR SENTENCE-LEVEL REVISION

- To improve the voice of the paper, ask the writer, "Do you talk like this?" Discuss the use of language in the paper, and then help the writer rework a small section and eliminate, for example, stuffiness or stilted words and phrases. To make the tone more appropriate in a formal paper, explain the conventions of formal writing. For example, explain that using contractions is inappropriate in a formal paper, as is the use of "etc."

- To eliminate wordiness, go through several sentences word by word with the writer to determine if each word is really necessary. You might also read wordy sentences back to the writer and then read the sentences again, leaving out what you think are excess words. Ask the writer to consider whether the words that you have omitted are necessary.

- To improve choppy writing, have the writer read the paper aloud. (Often, it is easier for the writer to detect choppiness when reading aloud than when reading silently.) You might want to have the writer revise some problem sentences in the tutoring session.

- If the writer tends to use several prepositional phrases in a row, read a few sentences aloud. As you read, accent the choppy effect that such phrases produce, and then show the writer how to eliminate at least some of the phrases. For example, changing "Running in the morning on the track on the campus keeps one fit" to "A morning run on the campus track keeps one fit" makes the sentence less choppy and less wordy, yet retains the meaning.

- Ask the writer to check his work for overuse of *to be* verb forms (such as *am, is, are, were*). He can improve emphasis by replacing these forms with more vigorous verbs and eliminating passive-voice constructions. If you notice that the writer overuses *to be* forms and the passive voice, ask him to circle all the verbs in a passage and then look at them and tell you what he notices. Alternatively, you and the writer might highlight all verbs in a paragraph so that he can see clearly how many of them are weak.

- For any of these sentence-level issues, take one of the writer's sentences, one of your own creation, or one from an exercise and demonstrate how making appropriate changes renders it more effective. Called *modeling*, this technique allows you to create several alternatives and to explain your reasoning for the changes.

Editing for Grammar, Punctuation, and Mechanics

After revising, we proofread, looking for typographical errors, omitted words, and other mistakes that we might have missed earlier. Remember Miguel, who asked his online tutor to "edit the punctuation" in the paper for his business writing class? He needs help with the editing stage, but rather than make the changes for him, the tutor can help Miguel identify error patterns, model one or two corrections, and encourage him to look for the same errors elsewhere in his paper.

It is important to remember that many writers often use catchphrases like *editing* or *proofreading* when asking for help, simply because those are familiar terms. Consequently, writers like Miguel who ask tutors to "edit" or "proofread" their papers may indeed need help with global revision, too.

When writers are ready for the editing (or proofreading) stage, tutors often worry that they must be thoroughly familiar with grammar rules, but that is not true. Good readers usually recognize a problem, though they may not always be able to explain it technically. If you are unsure about a rule or term, check an online or print guide to grammar, punctuation, and mechanics. Another handy and excellent reference that should not be overlooked is another tutor.

When you encounter problems with grammar, punctuation, or mechanics, paint a larger picture for writers. Explain that such errors distract readers from the paper's content. If readers pause to notice misplaced commas or misspellings, they lose the thread of the subject for a moment and must reorient themselves to continue reading. In the process, the paper's content may become less compelling.

As you discuss grammatical points, be flexible with your vocabulary. What one writer knows as a "fused" sentence another calls a "run-on." In addition, writers may be unfamiliar with terms like *comma splice* or *independent clause*. When you use technical terms, ask the writer if she needs a definition of the term or further clarification. If you are tutoring online and use a technical term, consider embedding a link with the definition and explanation of the term.

In *Teaching One-to-One: The Writing Conference*, Muriel Harris suggests turning the process of understanding over to writers by offering enough explanation to start them off and then inviting them to "find and revise all instances of whatever problem was discussed, asking questions as they proceed; to reformulate the principle for themselves in terms that they are comfortable with; to write their own sentences demonstrating the rule; to cite uses of the rule in their own papers if that seems helpful; or to explain how the rule works in their sentence."[3] If serious problems with grammar, punctuation, and mechanics permeate a student's paper, concentrate on a small section — a paragraph or several sentences — to help the writer recognize and learn to correct these errors. Later, the writer can go through the rest of the paper and apply what he has learned.

OTHER SUGGESTIONS FOR EDITING GRAMMAR, PUNCTUATION, AND MECHANICS

- Have writers read their papers aloud. In doing so, they often make corrections as they go, for the ear frequently judges more accurately than the eye. In addition, their changes afford you the opportunity to encourage them by pointing out that they really do know how to recognize and correct some of their errors.

- Point to an error and ask a general question, such as "Do you see a problem here?" You might underline several sentences that reflect the same problem and ask the writer to read them aloud. If the writer cannot see the problem, focus on a single sentence. If she still remains uncertain, explain the error and see if she can identify it elsewhere.

- Ask writers to indicate which sentences they feel uncomfortable with and then ask why.

COPING WITH THE LONG PAPER

Sometimes, writers find the task of writing a longer paper daunting. When they cannot complete the paper in one or two sittings, they become overwhelmed by the task. As a tutor, you can offer suggestions not only for planning, organizing, and writing but also for coping with the process in general. Chapter 7 offers some additional guidelines for tutoring longer papers.

- Briefly discuss the writer's writing process with him. When is the writer's optimum time for accomplishing a writing task? Early morning, when he is fresh? Late at night, so he can continue working if inspiration strikes? Help the writer to determine the best time to work and to plan accordingly.

- Help the writer break the larger task of "writing the paper" into a series of smaller, more easily achievable tasks. The list might begin as follows: Determine a broad or tentative topic, research to see what material is avail-

---

[3]Muriel Harris. *Teaching One-to-One: The Writing Conference.* Urbana: NCTE, 1986, 120.

able, reassess the topic and narrow it, draft an introduction, roughly outline the rest of the paper, and so on. Then, discuss planning each working session — research or writing — as another list of tasks, ones that can be accomplished within that time. The idea is to plan for achieving a sense of accomplishment and progress. In two hours, for example, it is doubtful that the writer will finish the paper, but she can think through and draft an introduction, then sketch out roughly what the rest of the paper might look like. Accomplishing these smaller goals allows the writer to feel some measure of success and progress.

- Offer specific suggestions to make each writing session successful. For example, many of us procrastinate by doing tasks that enable us to avoid writing. Suggest that writers set a time limit for working — a kind of contract with themselves — and stick to it: "I will work from 7:00 to 10:00 P.M." The promise of a reward at the end — updating a social media page, watching a television show, or eating a bowl of ice cream — increases the incentive to keep working.

- Suggest that when writers finish working for the day, they take a few moments to plan the subsequent session. Deciding where to begin next gives the following session direction from the outset and enables writers to start work immediately.

- Remind writers that writing is a process. They should pay attention initially to larger issues of content and organization, leaving concerns about sentence length and variety, spelling, punctuation, and the like for later.

WORKING WITH A TEXT DIGITALLY

Many writers may prefer to revise directly at the computer, either on their own laptops or on writing center computers. Working with a text digitally certainly has its benefits — the writer can revise without erasing, scribbling out, or trying to fit new thoughts or ideas in cramped spaces above and below the existing text. However, tutoring at the computer also requires special considerations, including the need to save multiple drafts, turn on Track Changes, and make effective use of white space and formatting commands.

Saving Multiple Drafts

Encourage writers to save multiple, dated versions of their work instead of overwriting a single draft again and again. These earlier drafts provide a tangible record of how far a writer has come since the beginning of the writing process and may be useful if a professor wants a look at past drafts to ensure that the paper is entirely the writer's own work.

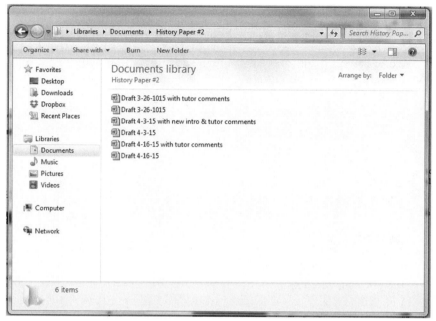

Saving Multiple Drafts

Revisiting earlier drafts may also inspire new ways of thinking as a writer struggles with a current draft. Is there a forgotten insight that might be expanded? Could an idea or point that was dropped initially be reintegrated into the current draft? Asking such questions may lead the writer to consider the current draft or some ideas for it in new ways.

Before you begin working on a draft with a writer, save the draft in a clear way—for example, "Writer's last name_WritingCenterDraft_11.13.15"—to ensure that there is a record of what the writer and you worked on together.

Turning on Track Changes

Most word processing programs have a reviewing or editing function that allows writers to track changes throughout the text. When you tutor at the computer, be sure to turn on Track Changes under the Review tab so that your work with the writer on the draft is clearly documented. Track Changes can also be a helpful way to record ideas and comments as you and the writer read through the paper together; writers can insert comments to help remember the major points that you discuss in the tutoring session. These comments will appear in the margins and are thus easily distinguishable from the rest of the text. Importantly, using Track Changes ensures that the final decision on any given revision is the writer's, not the tutor's, and gives the writer time for further reflection on the revisions after the tutoring session.

Making Use of White Space

Using the Return or Enter key, writers can break up their papers into distinct sections—sentences or paragraphs. This separation allows them to concentrate on smaller units and to see problems that sometimes get lost in standard prose. In this way, you and the writer can look at matters of style (like sentence length and variety), coherence (like transitions from one sentence to another), and syntax (like fragments, comma splices, run-on sentences, and parallelism). By isolating whole paragraphs, you and the writer can look specifically at the sentence order in each paragraph to consider rearranging them for coherence.

Writers can also double or even triple space to gain room to insert comments, options, or definitions above or below the appropriate place in the text. Writers can insert a revised version of part of the text above or below the original to compare and choose. They can also leave large blank spaces in appropriate spots as a reminder for the places where the essay needs further development.

Using Formatting Commands

To make writers more aware of their writing patterns, you can use a variety of formatting commands, such as highlight, underline, or **bold**. For example, you

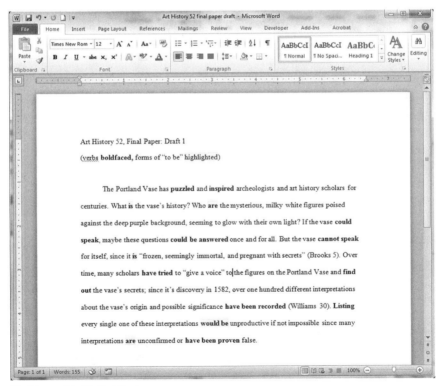

Working with Digital Text

can ask a writer who overuses forms of the verb *to be* to highlight all verbs in a portion of her text. You can then explain how to rephrase or combine sentences in order to achieve more vigor and variety. Similarly, when you discuss the need to provide support for ideas, you can ask the writer to highlight the main idea or topic sentence in each paragraph. She can then see if each remaining sentence in the paragraph supports that idea.

The writer can also use cut-and-paste commands to isolate the main idea (a key phrase) from each paragraph. After moving these key phrases to the end of the text, the writer can create a kind of outline of the paper. From there, you and the writer can consider such matters as the thesis statement, organization, coherence, and evidence.

The following exercises allow you to explore the writing process in several different ways: by considering how others describe the stages, by looking at how writing is taught at your school, by examining the language people use to talk about writing, and by taking a close look at your own writing process. You may do the exercises independently or in conjunction with a training course, and they can provide good starting points for group discussion.

EXERCISE 3A: Exploring How Writing Is Taught

How are writing and the writing process taught at your school? To answer this question, you should explore a variety of resources. The following list offers suggestions for questions to answer and ways to go about this task. You may wish to do this exercise in small groups, working together or dividing up the tasks.

- *Courses.* What writing courses are offered? Are they face-to-face, online, or hybrid courses? Are there special courses for English language learners? For basic writers or those less prepared to take a standard composition course? For honors students? Are there classes in intermediate or advanced composition? Are there courses in business or technical writing or other specialized areas? Are some courses sequential? Are there writing intensive courses?

Shoe-New Business: © 1982 Jim MacNelly. Distributed by King Features Syndicate, Inc.

- *Course descriptions.* Are there written descriptions of these courses? Often, school catalogs include short descriptions, but some writing programs offer more expanded explanations of the purpose and goals for each course. How does one course differ from another?

- *Textbooks and handbooks.* What textbooks (guides to writing, readers, style manuals, online materials) and handbooks are being used at your school? Your writing center or writing program office may have copies that you can examine, or you might check the shelves in the school bookstore or locate them online. Look through these texts. How are they organized? Make a list of the terms that they use to describe the stages of the writing process, and compare and contrast the ways in which they describe the stages. Set up the comparisons in the way that works best for you. You may want to sketch out your own informal chart.

- *Syllabi.* Does each writing course have a standard syllabus, or do teachers create their own? Check to see if your writing center or writing program office has a file of sample syllabi or if sample syllabi are posted online. If not, you might ask several teachers for copies. What kinds of assignments are included? Do they follow a particular sequence? How do instructors incorporate textbook or online material into their courses?

- *Assignments.* How are assignments given? Are they taken from the textbooks? Do teachers provide descriptions explaining the assignments? To answer these questions, you might poll several instructors, or you might check to see if there is a file of typical assignments.

- *Technology.* Is technology a part of writing classes? How is it incorporated in writing instruction? Do some or all classes meet online or in a smart classroom or computer lab? How—and how widely—do writing classes use the lab? How do classes and assignments use web environments and digital technology?

- *Competency exams.* Do any of the writing courses at your school use competency exams? Are they given during the course or at the end? What format(s) do they follow? What aspects of writing do they stress? If your writing center does not have a file of competency tests, try to get copies of old tests or practice tests from instructors. You may also want to talk to instructors about how and why they use them.

- *Writing-intensive courses.* Are there writing-intensive courses, perhaps as part of a writing-across-the-curriculum (WAC) or a writing-in-the-disciplines (WID) program? What defines these classes as being writing intensive? Are there guidelines for these classes? What are they like? What, if any, writing textbooks (perhaps a handbook or style manual) do they use?

- *Portfolios.* Do students put together portfolios of their work in any class, perhaps for evaluation? How many and what kind of materials are included in the portfolio? Are they sequential or themed?

EXERCISE 3B: Understanding Common Terms of the Writing Process

When writers meet with tutors, they use a variety of terms to discuss their writing. Many students echo their teachers and the ways that writing is discussed in their classes.

The following is a list of common writing terms with which you should be familiar. Define the ones that you already know, and then use textbooks and other resources from your school's writing program or writing center to define the rest.

Audience	Format	Rubric
Brainstorming	Freewriting	Subject-verb agreement
Coherence	Heuristics	Thesis
Comma splices	Invention	Tone
Composing process	Mechanics	Topic sentence
Digital	Multimodal	Voice
Emphasis	Organization	
Final draft	Point of view	
First draft	Revision	

The preceding list of terms is by no means exhaustive, for we commonly use many other terms as we discuss writing. Make a list of additional terms (with definitions) that might be used to discuss writing in your writing center. Your school may base its writing instruction on a particular textbook or approach to teaching writing, and you will need to be familiar with terms particular to that book or approach. Tutors at the University of Maryland Writing Center, for example, would add several terms from classical rhetoric—like *ethos*, *logos*, and *pathos*—because many writing teachers at that school use these terms in their classes.

EXERCISE 3C: Developing a Handout

Individually or in small groups, develop a handout or online resource that you and other tutors might use with writers. The handout may offer help with a stage of the writing process, discussing, for example, prewriting techniques, or it may explain and offer an exercise for a grammatical point. As you work, keep your audience firmly in mind. Make sure that your explanations are clear and complete and that your vocabulary is appropriate for the writers with whom you work. Do not make the mistake of one tutor, a sports buff, who in an effort to generate interest developed an exercise using sports jargon; writers unfamiliar with some terms found the exercise confusing.

EXERCISE 3D: The Writing Process in Action: Self-Reflection and Writer Case Study

Because you have been writing for many years, you have some ideas about what works (and what does not work) for you when you confront a writing task. But you have probably never taken a formal look at what you actually do from the moment you are given an assignment to the moment you hand it in. Exercise 3D asks you to write a paper in which you reflect on your writing process; Exercise 3E builds on that assignment by asking you to discuss and reflect on your experiences being tutored.

Choose one of the following topics, and write an essay of three to five pages. Meet with writing center tutors for assistance at least twice as you work on your paper. You may go at any time during your writing process, but work with two different tutors.

Topic 1: How I Write. We all go about writing in idiosyncratic ways. We find what works for us and what does not; then, we try to capitalize on the former and minimize the latter. Your task in this paper is to examine and discuss your own writing process. You may describe how you go about writing in general, or you may focus on a piece of writing that you have completed recently. As you compose, keep in mind that writing should delight as well as instruct. Consider other tutors to be your audience, and use the following questions as a guide:

- When you are confronted with a writing task, how do you approach it? Do you spend days fretting about it? Immediately jot down ideas and then start playing with them? Perform an online search of relevant terms to get an idea of what's out there? Think for days and then produce a first draft in one sitting?

- How do you go about producing a draft? Do you carefully assemble specific materials—like three sharp pencils and a legal-size pad? Don comfortable clothes—perhaps a favorite sweatshirt—and sit down at your laptop? Create an introduction that "will suffice" and then rework it later? Write, pace the floor a bit, write again, pace again?

- Do you write with the advice of a particular person—maybe a former teacher—echoing in your mind as you compose?

- When do you begin to consciously consider your audience? From the outset? As you revise your first draft? Do you seek advice as you write? Do you talk to others about your ideas and perhaps about how you organize them? Do you read to or show people drafts or parts of drafts? What kinds of feedback do you look for? When others give you suggestions, how do you factor them in?

- How do you feel when you have completed a paper? Are you simply glad that it is done? Are you convinced that one more pass would produce a better paper?

Topic 2: Writing Autobiography. How did you become the writer you are now? In this paper, your task is to explore your history as a writer. Consider the following questions as you plan your paper. Though you need not answer all of the questions, use them as prompts to stimulate your thinking about your engagement with writing and about your writing process.

- When did you begin writing? How old were you, what did you write about, and how did you go about it? How have innovations in technology changed the way you think or approach writing tasks?

- As you matured, how did your writing and the ways you went about it change? Did anyone or anything influence your writing? If so, who or what, and how?

- What kinds of writing do you do now or have you done? Have you written a diary or journal? Letters to a pen pal or family members? E-mail, blogs, Twitter entries, social media postings, or other online venues?

- What are your favorite and least favorite aspects of the writing process? What could you do to make your writing more effective?

- How do you see writing fitting into your life, both formally and informally, in the future?

Topic 3: Writer Case Study. Interview a writer—another tutor, a roommate, a friend—asking him or her the questions under Topic 1 and Topic 2. What do you find particularly interesting about the writer's process and development as a writer? Additionally, ask the writer for two to three essays that represent his or her writing. Read through the essays—do you see any consistent patterns of error? What are the writer's strengths? Where are there areas for improvement? With your knowledge of the writer's process and history, can you draw some tentative conclusions or make any conjectures as you read through the papers?

Discussion: Each of these three topics offers an ideal departure point for group discussion. If possible, meet with a group of tutors and read your papers aloud, or post your papers online for others to read and comment on. Compare and contrast the different ways you each go about a writing task. You will probably find a variety of approaches among members of your group. As others share, take notes—first, to pick up some hints for making your own process more efficient and, second, to begin compiling suggestions that you might offer students who seek your help.

EXERCISE 3E: Reflecting on Being Tutored

Shift your attention to the two tutoring sessions that you had as you completed exercise 3D. One of the best ways to discover how people feel about an experience is to put yourself in their shoes. You are learning to be a tutor, but you have just had the experience of sitting in the other chair—that of the writer being tutored—twice. Reflect on the following questions. You can attach your answers to your essay for 3D; additionally, you can discuss your answers with other tutors in a group setting.

- How did you feel about getting help from a tutor?
- What did the tutor do or suggest that you found helpful, in terms of both completing your assignment and making you feel more comfortable about getting help with your writing?
- Conversely, what, if anything, did the tutor do or say that confused you or made you feel uncomfortable?

4

The Writers You Tutor

Consider the diversity of the tutors in your writing center. Most likely you come from different geographic regions, represent an array of family backgrounds, and bring multiple cultural perspectives to your writing center. And this diversity is also reflected in your composing practices. In discussions with other tutors or friends, you have likely noted both interesting similarities and stark differences in your writing processes.

Similarly, the writers you tutor will have varied learning styles, attitudes, backgrounds, and competencies that affect how they process information and approach their writing assignments. Some writers have writing anxieties or learning disabilities; others may be multilingual and learning English as a second (or third or fourth) language. You will probably tutor writers with a broad range of K–12 experiences, and some may be less prepared for the kinds of writing college demands. Knowing specific approaches or strategies for assisting these writers can make sessions with them more beneficial and productive. Keep in mind that there is not one model or default "good" writer, that all writers—the nineteen-year-old; the older, returning student; the part-time student; the self-identified multilingual student; the first-generation college student—bring to the writing center compelling stories and unique needs.

We think you will find the suggestions and approaches in this chapter useful in tutoring all writers. Indeed, we encourage you to apply the concept of "universal design" to tutoring writing. Sometimes new tutors think they must conduct sessions differently for those with identifiably labeled "differences," but that's not really the case. What the architectural term *universal design* teaches us is that products, the built environment, and services can be pleasing to and usable by everyone, regardless of age, ability, or other differences. In tutoring writing, it means that every session focuses foremost on assisting a writer with her writing. A part of doing that takes differences into

account, but as accommodations and not as something that defines the writer.[1]

Along those lines, we have another suggestion that bears special mention because it applies to working with any writer who seeks help from a writing tutor: Regard and discuss the paper that the writer presents as a rough draft. The term *rough draft* can apply to a spectrum of writing in the drafting and revising process, including notes, loosely organized paragraphs, or even the writer's fourth revision. Regardless of how messy or clean the draft is, think and talk about it as a work in progress, one that is full of promise and potential. This stance allows you to discuss aspects of the paper in terms of what might be *more effective* instead of what is *inadequate* or *wrong*.

Writers do not always think of their papers as drafts, and while they may request suggestions for improvement, they may not be immediately receptive to your advice. Though they may not articulate or even recognize it, their writing is quite personal and sharing it can make them feel vulnerable. Their drafts represent authorial decisions they have made, which can lead to their taking criticism more personally than it is intended. This sensitivity can be particularly acute for first or early drafts, the likes of which may present many areas for improvement. As a tutor, try to frame the negative aspects of a paper as good first steps toward improvement and offer lots of encouragement. For example, a paper may lack organization but present several good ideas. Start with those good ideas and help the writer reorganize. Or, the writer may make a claim that is unsubstantiated. Praise her for the interesting claim, but then ask her to provide more support for that claim. Furthermore, point to successful aspects of the paper in order to encourage and support the writer. Perhaps you can point to a specific focus, places where the audience is particularly well considered, or an enticing introduction. Explain that the draft accomplishes much that is good and promising, and then enumerate those aspects.

How much nicer to treat the paper as a draft and discuss its potential than to regard it as a final copy and offer only negative comments! Praise and affirmation always feel good; we like to hear that we've attempted something and done it well, even as we recognize that we could do it better. Feeling successful in some areas allows writers to more easily continue working to improve

---

[1]Dinitz, Sue. "Changing Notions of Difference in the Writing Center: The Possibilities of Universal Design" (with Jean Kiedaisch). *The Writing Center Journal* 27.2 (2007): 39–59.

in other areas, and places tutors in a perfect position to facilitate and encourage writers, especially those who struggle. It is also worthwhile to remind ourselves that learning styles and cultural background, as well as events in daily life, affect the ways each of us handles a writing assignment. You might never know about some of these influences (a writer's concerns about family or financial problems, for example), but it is important to be aware that such concerns may exist. As you work with individuals, your words and actions should convey sensitivity and understanding; each writer deserves to be treated fairly and with respect.

LEARNING STYLES

In previous chapters, you looked at the ways in which you and other tutors complete writing tasks. You doubtlessly discovered that each person has a different approach, and the same is true of the ways we learn. We tend to assume that others learn the way we do and are sometimes mystified when explanations or approaches that make perfect sense to us do not click with them. But not everyone absorbs and retains information in the same way, and different writers respond to different tutoring strategies.

At the most basic level, people learn by seeing (visual), by hearing (auditory), and by doing (kinesthetic, which is the Greek word for *movement*). Usually, writers are aware of their personal learning styles and can communicate to you how they best learn. Remember that people retain more of what they learn when they are actively involved and engaged in the process. With some writers, it may be appropriate to ask if they learn best by seeing, hearing, or doing. If you have trouble getting through to a writer with one technique—say, simply talking over a draft—you might want to try another approach, perhaps jotting down notes, creating an informal outline, or drawing diagrams. As you become more familiar with the writers who visit your writing center and have a chance to try different approaches, you will gain a better sense of what they respond to best.

Visual Strategies

- Rather than simply talking, work from written material, pointing to, circling, highlighting, or otherwise indicating information as you discuss it.
- Make writing things down a part of the tutoring session by taking notes, jotting down examples, or drawing diagrams. When writers leave, they will have something to take along—visual reminders of what you have discussed with them.
- Use color when possible, with colored pens or, if working on the computer, by highlighting or choosing colors for fonts when inserting new text.

- Separate a passage into individual sentences on the computer and use some of the other suggestions in "Working with a Text Digitally" in Chapter 3.

Auditory Strategies

- Read instructions, notes, or other materials aloud, or have writers read aloud.
- Repeat or rephrase directions and explanations, especially ones that may be more complicated.
- Verbally reinforce points made in notes, diagrams, or other visual aids.
- Throughout the session, ask the writer to paraphrase what you have discussed; at the end of the session, ask the writer to summarize what was accomplished and outline his plan for the paper.
- Suggest that the writer record the session on her phone or other device.
- If working online in real-time, record the session; if working online asynchronously, consider using software to embed an audio file to supplement your written advice.

Kinesthetic Strategies

- As you read through papers or discuss ideas, ask students to do the writing, underlining, highlighting, or diagramming.
- Have writers point to material as you talk about it.
- Write sentences or sections of a paper on sticky notes, separate pieces of paper, or file cards—or even cut the writer's draft into parts. Ask the writer to rearrange the sentences or passages to find the most effective organization.
- Have sticky notes on hand, and use them to identify parts of the paper, like the thesis, topic sentences, and evidence. Have the student write the concept on the sticky note and then match it to the appropriate part of the paper.

STUDENT CONCERNS

If you have ever tried to write a paper after a fight with your parents or a close friend, when you are frantic about another course, or when coping with a difficult roommate, then you know that writing can be influenced by factors in your life other than school.

The following chart shows some common concerns of college students. As you look through it, think about the writers who come to the writing center. Consider that, at various times, writers may have additional anxieties. For example, first-year or transfer students are adapting to a new school; many sophomores are choosing a major; seniors are facing job searches and increased independence; and returning students are coping with school, family, and job responsibilities. Though you cannot—and would not want to—be privy to all of their concerns, it is good to remind yourself of the various personal issues that can affect students' writing.

ACADEMIC CONCERNS

Competition	Study skills	Classes (size, difficulty)
Grades	Test anxiety	School size, bureaucracy
Family's or personal expectations		

SOCIAL CONCERNS

Roommates	Separation from family and friends
Friendships	Dating and relationships
Sexuality	Peer pressure

LIFESTYLE CONCERNS

Independence	Living arrangements	Privacy
Job responsibilities	Finances	Family issues
Health concerns		

Below, we offer specific strategies with working with specific populations of writers. Allow us to reiterate what we stated at the top of this chapter: First, we hope that you will see the value in using these strategies with *all* writers, and, second, we advise you to take care not to make assumptions based on your initial and limited perceptions of the writers who enter your writing center. Remember that literacy practices—written and oral—are richly varied. Perhaps there will come a day when universities and colleges will value all of these literacy practices equally, but, at present, the reality is that standard academic English still reigns. Therefore, part of your job as a tutor is to help writers gain increased competence and confidence in standard academic English. Moreover, if you are a tutor who identifies with any of the categories below, then you have the added benefit of experience—if you wish, you may share your own frustrations, challenges, and successes with tutors and writers. And if you have additional strategies to add to the repertoire below, we are sure that they will be welcome in your writing center!

THE WRITER WITH WRITING ANXIETY

Kathy panics the moment she hears the words "write a paper." Rather than take notes as the teacher gives instructions, she tunes out the details and thinks only about the monumental task of producing a paper. As she leaves class, Kathy frantically asks her classmates, "What are we supposed to do?

Calvin and Hobbes   by Bill Watterson

How long is it? When is it due?" Kathy has writing anxiety, which can take many forms. One writer frets because he cannot produce a polished piece of writing in one sitting. Another writer dislikes writing so much that he puts off getting down to work and finds himself approaching the deadline with little behind him but worry and procrastination. Still another writes and writes and writes, disheartened that she cannot get what she has to say "right."

Though the specific suggestions that you offer each of these writers may vary, it is always helpful to present yourself as a sympathetic ally. When Daniel first came to the writing center, he described himself as "desperate." "Why can't I just sit down and write?" he asked. "Isn't that what everyone else does?" As he discussed his concerns with a tutor, she shared her own frustrations about writing, and Daniel began to see that he was not alone. They worked together on his next few papers, and with his tutor's help, Daniel figured out ways of addressing his writing anxiety so that he could become more productive and confident. Eventually, Daniel decided that helping others with their writing would be rewarding — and would also help him develop even stronger skills — and he became a writing tutor himself. He was an especially good tutor because he understood the insecurities many writers face.

Likewise, you might tell students about some of your writing frustrations. Acknowledge that writing is indeed hard work, not only for them but for everyone. Telling students that experienced writers often find it difficult to sit down and apply themselves can be surprisingly reassuring. Sharing details about the messiness of your own early drafts — the rambling introduction that suffices early on, the misspellings and poor grammar that you'll fix later — grants writers permission to be imperfect as well, and to show and discuss their own tentative drafts without apology. But you should also tell them that the satisfaction of producing a well-written paper is enormously rewarding.

SOME SUGGESTIONS FOR WORKING WITH A WRITER WHO HAS WRITING ANXIETY

- Briefly explain the writing process. Point out that beginning as soon as possible and allowing plenty of time actually makes the task easier.

Getting words on paper helps writers figure out what they want to say. Starting early also allows time for the unconscious mind to play with the ideas that have consciously been gathered.

- Help writers break the assignment into a sequence of specific, manageable tasks, and then help them set up a reasonable schedule with deadlines for completing the various parts. Consider putting these deadlines into a calendar that you print for the writer. This planning will also enable writers to schedule and make use of the writing center throughout the writing process, which can prevent small problems from becoming big ones.

- Point out that breaking down the process of writing a paper into specific, manageable tasks can help writers feel degrees of success along the way. Rather than planning to sit down for an evening to "write the paper," a writer might set out to draft an introduction and work out a tentative organization for the rest of the paper or plan to revise a particular section of the paper. Approaching tasks in this way enables writers to leave their desks with a sense of having accomplished what they set out to do, rather than with disappointment or frustration that the paper is not yet finished after several hours of work.

- Suggest that writers set firm writing appointments with themselves and build in rewards. They can promise to work for a set period without interruptions and then get a reward at the end—a bike ride, a new music download, or some other treat. Such rewards may sound silly, but the strategy often works.

- Remind writers that a rough draft is exactly that: rough. Especially in the early stages, writing needs to be free flowing rather than perfect. Writers should be concerned with putting ideas on paper and not get bogged down with finding the "right" word or making each sentence perfect before beginning the next one.

THE WRITER WITH BASIC WRITING SKILLS

In *Errors and Expectations*, Mina Shaughnessy illuminates the difficulties that writers with basic writing skills may have in producing effective academic writing. In this landmark book, Shaughnessy describes basic writers' challenges with handwriting, punctuation, syntax, grammar, and spelling and then discusses the difficulties caused by their lack of familiarity with the concepts and forms of academic writing. Throughout this book and in her other publications about basic writing, Shaughnessy addresses teachers' attitudes, underscoring the importance of respecting basic writers' intelligence. She makes the point that basic writers are as capable as any other student, but may struggle with a lack of information or misinformation. Shaughnessy explains that these writers do not necessarily apply grammatical rules incorrectly but instead use a different set of rules, acquired from speaking the English of their home communities.[2]

Since Shaughnessy wrote *Errors and Expectations,* a robust body of scholarship has emerged that addresses basic writing in the context of literacy practices and the sociocultural factors that inform those practices. If you will be tutoring basic writers frequently, probably the best way to prepare is to consult the many resources available through the Council on Basic Writing.

SOME SUGGESTIONS FOR WORKING WITH BASIC WRITERS

- Take care to be supportive, respectful, patient, and encouraging. Writers with basic writing skills often feel especially frustrated and even defeated by the task of writing. Be sure to acknowledge (and thus reinforce) what they do well, whether it's a larger issue like organization or a smaller issue like an especially appropriate phrase or word.

- Talk with writers about their perceptions of writing and of the writing process. Help them understand that the writing process moves from the messy, tentative beginnings of formulating and ordering ideas to getting those ideas on paper and making meaning of them, first for the writer and then for the reader. By discussing the larger process, you reassure writers that they do not have to produce perfectly formed ideas and writing from the start. When you explain the editing stage, emphasize that this stage ensures that errors will not distract readers.

- Help writers develop and convey meaning by explaining what you think they said in a sentence or passage. For example, after reading a concluding paragraph, you might say, "Your last paragraph says that you've shown four ways students can reduce stress, but I remember only three: [list them]. Did I miss one? Can you show me where it is?" By responding to writers in this way, you can help them see where the meaning of their writing does not match their intentions.

- Look at grammar and punctuation not in isolation but as a part of communicating ideas effectively. If writers struggle to combine two sentences, use that example to talk about the appropriate punctuation rather than simply handing them an exercise on commas or semicolons. Also, explain to writers that grammatical mistakes tend to distract readers from the content, leaving them to wonder "Should there be a comma here?" or "Does this verb agree with the subject?" instead of attending to the writer's message.

- Have writers read their papers aloud or into a digital recorder. Listening to themselves can help writers identify weaknesses in development, coherence,

---

[2]Mina Shaughnessy. *Errors and Expectations.* New York: Oxford University Press, 1979.

and sentence structure. This activity also reinforces and encourages writers' ability to recognize their own weaknesses—and their strengths.

- Do not overwhelm writers with too much information or too many suggestions at once. It is better to cover one or two areas well so that writers can master them and feel successful. You can acknowledge other problems, but address them in later sessions.

- If a writer has several writing concerns, work with her to develop a strategy for coping with them. Make a plan for the next paper(s) and how to deal with grammatical and mechanical issues. Suggest that the writer see a tutor early and regularly throughout the writing process.

- You might begin with a session to clarify the assignment (purpose, scope, audience) and then schedule other sessions to work through prewriting, drafting parts of the paper, and revising—all according to the writer's needs. Likewise, list the other issues to attend to, prioritize them, make a plan of attack, and schedule future sessions. Be realistic, and do not overwhelm the writer. You might arrange to split each session between working on the paper and working on these other issues.

THE MULTILINGUAL WRITER

Tutors and writers alike bring a rich variety of linguistic and cultural experiences to the writing center, and no one term appropriately encompasses or addresses all multilingual writers or reflects the complexity of English language acquisition. As a writing tutor, you will likely have the privilege of working with such writers across a wide spectrum of cultures, experiences, and expertise. One writer may have been born in a particular country like the United States, but speaks a heritage language—such as Spanish or Chinese—in her neighborhood community; another writer may be foreign-born and earning his degree in an English-speaking country; still another writer may have received her formal schooling in two languages and is adjusting to English-only instruction. Perhaps you also are a multilingual writer working in the writing center. If so, you understand that becoming proficient in a language can be a slow process, and sensitivity to linguistic and cultural diversity is crucial to a successful tutoring session. Indeed, unfamiliar customs and ways of thinking may be reflected in the writing of multilingual writers or in their approaches to the writing process. Culture determines acceptable ways of presenting information, and in a tutoring session, acknowledging cultural differences often means explaining appropriate rhetorical patterns for standard academic English.

In some cultures, for example, the welfare of the group is more important than that of the individual, and the notion of individuals owning ideas may seem strange. Western cultures, however, embrace the individual and insist on careful attribution and documentation in written texts. Consequently, you may need to be sensitive to how you address academic integrity and frame your explanations within the unique rhetorical context of your university. Likewise, Americans tend to value a direct approach, but some cultures privilege more implied methods. One culture may lean toward exaggeration and emotionalism; another may do quite the opposite, focusing on restraint and understatement. These cultural differences often influence the rhetorical choices multilingual writers make in terms of content and strategies when they are writing in English. For example, writers from non-Western cultures not only may have difficulty conceptualizing how to write for a Western audience—with emphases on thesis and argument as well as on conciseness and clarity—but also may be unsure about how to function in a Western university. Such difficulties may be reflected in their writing. While you want to be aware of cultural differences, you should not assume that every writer you meet from a particular culture embodies what you know about that culture. What is important is that when you encounter these differences, you respect them for what they represent: unique ways of looking at the world.

Furthermore, the grammatical issues that multilingual writers deal with are not homogeneous; rather, they may depend on an individual's first language and on previous instruction and experience in English. A writer whose first language does not include articles, for instance, may well have difficulty knowing when to use *a*, *an*, or *the*. Many problems that multilingual writers encounter occur because their first language follows different rules: for example, prepositions may not function as they do in English, the same rules of subject-verb agreement may not apply, or adjectives may follow rather than precede nouns. Additionally, some multilingual writers work diligently to master rules for English usage and can cite and apply grammar rules correctly in an exercise but have difficulty applying them as they write an essay. To get an idea of what some multilingual writers face as they attempt to acquire a second language, look at the example of Arabic grammar on page 62.

A Simple Translation Can Be a Language Barrier

Translating any language is not simply a process of transferring individual words from one language to another. Arabic grammar structure, for example, is very different from English grammar structure. Word-for-word translation of a simple sentence may not convey the precise message and can lead to confusion.

In English, sentences always contain *both* a noun/subject *and* a verb/predicate; however, in Arabic, sentences may lack either the noun/subject or the verb/predicate. Arabic sentences are categorized into either verbal sentences or nominal sentences, depending on whether they start with the verb or the noun. A **verbal sentence** starts with a verb, and the subject usually comes after the verb. However, sometimes the subject is not included. It is either implied, or, if it is a pronoun, it is attached to the end of the verb. Take, for instance, the following example (be sure to read the Arabic from right to left!):

EXAMPLE ONE: VERBAL SENTENCE

- ## English:

Yesterday, I read an interesting story.

- ## Arabic:

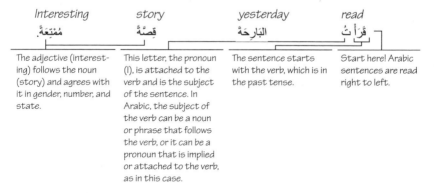

Interesting	story	yesterday	read
مُمْتِعَةٌ.	قِصَّةٌ	البَارِحَةَ	قَرَأْتُ
The adjective (interesting) follows the noun (story) and agrees with it in gender, number, and state.	This letter, the pronoun (I), is attached to the verb and is the subject of the sentence. In Arabic, the subject of the verb can be a noun or phrase that follows the verb, or it can be a pronoun that is implied or attached to the verb, as in this case.	The sentence starts with the verb, which is in the past tense.	Start here! Arabic sentences are read right to left.

A **nominal Arabic sentence** starts with a noun or pronoun. It has a subject and a predicate, which provides information about the subject. The predicate can be one word (noun or adjective), a phrase, or a sentence, but never a single verb. A nominal Arabic sentence is equivalent to an English simple sentence constructed with the verb "to be." For example, the following sentence in English contains the verb "is," a form of the infinitive verb "to be," but in the Arabic sentence the verb is implied.

EXAMPLE TWO: NOMINAL SENTENCE

- ## English:

The sky is clear.

- ## Arabic:

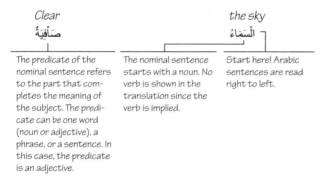

Clear	the sky
صَافِيَةٌ	الْسَمَاءُ
The predicate of the nominal sentence refers to the part that completes the meaning of the subject. The predicate can be one word (noun or adjective), a phrase, or a sentence. In this case, the predicate is an adjective.	The nominal sentence starts with a noun. No verb is shown in the translation since the verb is implied.	Start here! Arabic sentences are read right to left.

---

*Graphic representations and explanations on this page courtesy of Nabila Hijazi.

When you work with multilingual writers, respond first to the content and organization of their papers, as you would with any writer. Fixing sentences that may later be discarded wastes time. Read the description of the assignment and see if the paper adequately addresses the audience and fulfills the purpose. Listen to what writers are trying to say on paper and help them make sense of it.

Encourage writers to talk through what they want to say in each paragraph—in other words, to describe briefly each paragraph's focus and content. This nonevaluative approach is especially helpful with writers who are unaccustomed to questioning authority (and to them, you are the authority in the tutoring situation). As you work with writers and their papers, ask questions that will help you understand what they are trying to communicate. Paraphrase what they say to see if you understand it correctly.

Be aware, however, that some writers may regard you as an expert and expect you to provide answers and simply fix the problems in their papers, putting you at cross purposes with them. As you ask the open-ended questions that aim to make writers responsible for their papers, they may listen quietly, waiting to record answers. As Muriel Harris notes,

> [T]here may be a strained silence in a tutorial when a tutor asks and then waits patiently for answers to standard tutors' questions intended to give the students an active role, such as "How would you fix this paragraph?" or "What do you see as the problem here?" The tutor may interpret this silence as an indication that the student doesn't have an answer, but it may more likely be that the student is also sitting patiently, waiting for the tutor to fulfill his or her function of providing such answers. Some discussion is then necessary to help the student see that he or she really is being given an opportunity to learn by offering an answer.[3]

As you work with multilingual writers, remember that no one can absorb a great deal of information at one time. In fact, too much help can be overwhelming and can make writers feel even less secure. It is wiser to concentrate on one or two problems at a time so that writers can understand them and feel some degree of success. You can point out other problems, but leave them for subsequent tutoring sessions.

English can sometimes be illogical, and learning it can be difficult. As you work with writers, strike an appropriate balance between sympathy and encouragement. When multilingual writers are serious students who are unaccustomed to encountering difficulties with a course, they find their problems with writing in English especially frustrating. Even as you show

---

[3]Muriel Harris. "Cultural Conflicts in the Writing Center: Expectations and Assumptions of ESL Students" in *The St. Martin's Sourcebook for Writing Tutors*, 3rd ed. Ed. Christina Murphy and Steve Sherwood. Boston: Bedford/St. Martin's, 2008, 211.

understanding of their problems, take special care to reinforce what they do know, and encourage them to learn and apply rules.

SOME SUGGESTIONS FOR WORKING WITH MULTILINGUAL WRITERS

The most important qualities you can bring to tutoring sessions with multilingual writers are patience and respect, and you can communicate those qualities through your words and actions. Recognize the difficulty of what they are trying to accomplish and how hard they work at it. But don't stop there; learn from them and enjoy doing so! As you work with multilingual writers, consider the following suggestions:

- Beginning a tutoring session with a multilingual writer can have its own unique problems. Be aware that the writer may be especially apprehensive not only about showing you his writing but also about working with you. Take special care to establish a comfortable rapport at the beginning of a session. He may worry about talking with you in imperfect English or with an accent. Striking up an informal conversation may help allay fears and calm nerves, and talking easily about the paper may give you some information about the writer's questions and concerns.

- At the same time, be aware that another writer may regard this casual conversation as a waste of valuable time that could — or perhaps should — be spent more directly addressing issues of writing correctly. How to deal? You might try asking something like "We could talk for a few minutes about your paper and writing, and that would help me understand what your concerns are. Would that be okay?"

- Make an extra effort to put multilingual writers at ease. In some cultures, asking questions is impolite, so encourage writers to ask questions if they find your comments confusing or unclear.

- Give directions plainly. Watch writers' expressions, and ask questions to see if they comprehend your explanations. Multilingual writers may be too embarrassed to admit that they are unsure. They may smile and nod in agreement but still be confused. If you are not sure whether someone understands something, ask her to explain what you have said or to give you an example. Be patient and, if necessary, explain again.

- If a multilingual writer does not understand a comment or an explanation, rephrase it in different terms. Do not raise your voice or simply repeat the same words.

- If you have difficulty understanding a multilingual writer, watch for facial expressions as he speaks. The combination of watching and hearing can help you follow what the writer is saying.

- Many multilingual writers write better than they speak. Do not assume that because you have trouble understanding someone's speech, he will have significant problems with writing.

- Generally, writers should do most, or even all, of the writing in tutoring sessions; however, with some multilingual writers, handling all the tasks required in a tutoring session—listening, thinking, reading, speaking, writing—can be overwhelming. For example, when they are exploring ideas for a paper or talking through ways to organize those ideas, the tasks of listening, thinking, and expressing thoughts clearly may be enough for them. It may be helpful for you to serve as scribe, jotting down key words or phrases *in the writer's words*. At appropriate points, you can use these key phrases to help them start writing or express themselves more clearly. When the session ends, you can hand the writer these notes; to reinforce the notions that the paper is the writer's own and that she, indeed, has ideas and words to write it, point out that what's on the paper are her own words, expressions, and thoughts.

- Expecting a multilingual writer to be familiar with English phrases or idioms is sometimes unrealistic. Occasionally, you may need to supply an appropriate word or phrase and simply consider it "a gift."

- Plagiarism is not always the deliberate violation of rules that it seems. In Western cultures, we value originality in writing and regard a piece of writing as belonging to the person who produced it, so we cite the sources of borrowed ideas and words as we write, and we have rules with regard to how to avoid plagiarism. But not all cultures share these values. In some cultures, using another writer's words is a form of flattery, and multilingual writers may not comprehend the need to document sources clearly. Though you will need to explain Western academic rules and customs about citing sources and doing one's own work, be aware that multilingual writers may not be knowingly violating those rules.

- Try not to focus only on the mechanical and grammatical errors in the paper. In English language acquisition, grammatical correctness may take quite a while, and it is only through frequent practice—lots of writing—that a writer will gain proficiency. If you find a grammatical problem that impedes the readability of the paper, point to several places where it occurs and help the writer correct the errors. Then, ask the writer to find similar errors in the paper. This practice will help the writer become independent in his own editing.

Tutors tend to believe that they must be expert grammarians to work with multilingual writers, but that is not necessarily true. As Phyllis Brooks points out, "There is in the tradition of foreign languages and of English as a second language, a long tradition of the native informant: a sympathetic person who is literate and speaks well in his or her own language and can produce correct forms for students to imitate, or can suggest better forms for sentences than the student has tried, unsuccessfully, to produce."[4] Adults acquiring a new language rely heavily on imitation. You can help writers rephrase a sentence and produce other sentences of the same kind. Producing such examples establishes patterns that writers can begin to incorporate into their speaking and writing. You also need to know that you will not be able to explain everything or answer all multilingual writers' questions about why some phrases or grammatical constructions work in certain ways. Eventually, however, you will become familiar with — and better able to help multilingual writers correct — some basic kinds of grammatical and syntactical errors.

THE WRITER WITH A LEARNING DISABILITY

Some writers have problems perceiving or processing information; these cognitive problems interfere with their learning and writing. However, there is disagreement among experts with regard to the causes and treatments of these problems, and only a trained professional can definitively diagnose a learning disability. Even defining the term *learning disability* is difficult and controversial because the symptoms are merely clues: Some are clear-cut, while others are more subtle. Writers with learning disabilities may reverse letters, numbers, and even whole words — for example, seeing or writing *was* for *saw*. They may confuse concepts like up and down. Their handwriting may be difficult to read, and they may misspell words in inconsistent ways. It is important to remember, however, that writers with learning disabilities are not incapable of writing well; they simply process information in ways that can present additional challenges to the writing process.

Coping with a learning disability can be difficult for writers. They may be embarrassed, like the writer who whispers to his tutor that, unlike in high school, he had hoped to make it in college without special assistance and then asks the tutor to help him without letting his teacher know. Or the writer with a learning disability may become easily frustrated and shut down after not understanding a concept following several tries and seek the relief of a quick exit. As a tutor, you need to be sensitive to the feelings of these writers. Without being condescending, make them feel comfortable when asking for and receiving help.

Our discussion of learning styles at the beginning of this chapter is especially appropriate for tutoring writers with learning disabilities. They can usually tell you how they learn best and what you can do to make your comments

---

[4]Phyllis Brooks. "Peer Tutoring and the ESL Student" in *Improving Writing Skills: New Directions for College Learning Assistance*. Ed. Thom Hawkins and Phyllis Brooks. San Francisco: Jossey-Bass, 1981, 48.

and explanations most beneficial. In many cases, writers are aware of their disabilities and have learned to compensate. They know that they may need to take a test orally or with additional time, for example. If a writer tells you that he has a learning disability but does not offer information about coping strategies, ask. Work with these writers as conscientiously as you would with any writer, but take additional care to involve the writer, to structure and sequence material, and then to reinforce that structure. Above all, be patient!

SOME SUGGESTIONS FOR WORKING WITH WRITERS WITH LEARNING DISABILITIES

- Find a quiet place to work—one that minimizes distractions.
- Ask what you can do that will best help the writer, both in terms of an approach (perhaps an outline of the paper?) and in terms of tasks (should you, and not the writer, do the physical writing?). Teach to a writer's favored learning style. The earlier discussion of learning styles contains specific suggestions to help convey and reinforce information to a variety of people. You might want to be creative and try combining approaches.
- Be patient, explain things clearly, and repeat or rephrase if necessary.
- As you talk and go through the writer's notes or draft, make lists or outlines or notes that can later serve as guides or reminders for the writer. Toward the end of the session, you might review—and perhaps reorder—them with the writer.
- Remember that a writer with a learning disability often struggles very hard to accomplish what may come to others quite easily. Support, encouragement, and praise are especially important to a writer who is easily frustrated or discouraged, so take care to offer positive comments liberally where they are due.
- Be aware that a writer with a learning disability may correct something and then immediately repeat the same error. Do not assume that she is lazy or has not been paying attention.

THE WRITER WITH A PHYSICAL CHALLENGE

Giving writers with physical challenges access to tutoring means providing more than physical access to tutoring facilities. It involves using flexible and diverse approaches to make sure that each writer has the opportunity to learn in ways that work best for him or her.

Writers with physical challenges will usually tell you that they have special needs and will explain how you can most easily help them. Perhaps you should take notes, or sit in a particular place in relation to them, or help them position their computer so they can access their own assistive software. If they don't volunteer the information, ask them if there is anything specific that you can do to make the tutoring session more productive. If the explanation isn't completely clear to you, ask more questions for clarification.

In addition to listening, however, you also need to be observant. Throughout the session, pay special attention to see what's working and what perhaps should be modified. What is most important as you work with someone with a disability is to maintain a generosity of spirit and a wish to provide the best possible tutoring experience. Doing so means being flexible in offering, demonstrating, or reinforcing explanations; in determining who writes or reads during the session; and in deciding how long the session should be. Decisions should be made in the best interest of the writer, rather than according to the regular policies that you or your writing center may follow. Rigid time limits for a session, for example, may need to be relaxed to optimally accommodate a student with special needs. In any session, consider recording a session so that the writer can listen later. To reinforce what you discussed or to make new notes, he may want to listen later in a quieter setting.

As a general rule, when you work with visually or hearing impaired writers, speak naturally and clearly, using a normal tone of voice at a reasonable pace. Avoid the impulse to exaggerate your speech or raise your voice. Hearing impaired writers may communicate with you by lip reading, by writing notes, or by bringing an interpreter with them who can sign as you speak. As the two of you work, be sure to give the writer time to absorb meaning and ask questions; also include opportunities to review and clarify what has been covered.

SOME SUGGESTIONS FOR WORKING WITH WRITERS WHO ARE VISUALLY IMPAIRED

- Use technology. Technology has come a long way in assisting the visually impaired, and writers may use screen readers, screen enlargers, or other low vision devices to assist them with reading and writing. Many campus disability support services offer assistive software for free or at a reduced rate, and your writing center may be able to request that these tools be installed on writing center computers.

- Verbalize everything. People with partial sight can see some things and not others, and sometimes their vision will vary from day to day or hour to hour depending upon the lighting condition or eye fatigue. Some see well in or even prefer dim light, because bright light or glare may bother them. Verbalize everything as you work with and observe the writer in the session; don't presume to know what is best, but follow the writer's cues and revise your strategies according to what he indicates will work best for him.

- When you write on a piece of paper or a dry-erase board or whiteboard, print using dark colors and large letters.

- To diminish distractions, consider moving to a quieter place.

- It is fine to use words or phrases that refer to sight, like "see," "watch," or "look over here." Such words are also in the vocabulary of a blind student.

SOME SUGGESTIONS FOR WORKING WITH WRITERS WHO ARE HEARING IMPAIRED

- Face the writer and look directly at her as you speak. Remember not to speak when your back is toward the writer. Face the light, so you are not silhouetted against a bright window, for example.
- To facilitate lip reading, do not exaggerate your lip movements; doing so can make it more difficult to understand your speech. It is easier to lip read phrases and sentences than individual words. Let facial expressions and body language help to convey your message, but don't exaggerate them.
- When accommodating an interpreter, make sure the writer has an unobstructed view of both you and the interpreter. Speak directly to the writer and maintain eye contact with her. The interpreter will interpret your words directly. Look to the writer for a response; do not expect the sign language interpreter to answer for the writer.
- To avoid distraction and interference with auditory devices, keep noise to a minimum or move to a quieter area.
- Vision is the primary means of taking in information, so use a visual format. Reinforce auditory information by providing visual information. Write down key words, make notes and lists, and use other visual aids and materials. Ask the writer to take notes.
- Keep explanations brief and uncomplicated. Break information into small steps. As with any writer, use more than one way to demonstrate or explain information.

THE ADULT LEARNER

Most universities and colleges have an active adult learner population. Sometimes known as the *nontraditional* or *returning* student, the adult learner is a student who is returning to or beginning college several years after high school graduation. Adult learners return to college for a variety of reasons, including personal fulfillment, career changes, military discharge, and job promotion.

Adult learners typically have spouses, children, jobs, and bills to pay, and consequently must fit college into an already demanding life. Furthermore, because they may not have been in school for many years, they often have considerable anxieties about their scholarly aptitude and performance. Adult learners are often highly motivated; at the same time, they can be extremely demanding of themselves and, by extension, the tutor. Nonetheless, the tutoring session with an adult learner can be most rewarding, as she is often extremely attentive and receptive to tutors' advice.

SOME SUGGESTIONS FOR WORKING WITH ADULT LEARNERS

- Be considerate of the adult learner's time. The writer may have taken off work or skipped a daughter's basketball game to come to the writing center.
- Be sensitive to the writer's anxiety and supportive of his efforts to return to school despite the obstacles. Maintain an encouraging and empathetic tone.
- Be aware of age differences and your demeanor. If the person is your elder, she may expect you to demonstrate certain signs of respect and may appreciate a more formal tone in the tutoring session.
- Help writers use real-world experience appropriately in their academic papers. Adult learners come with a vast amount of professional and personal experience, and they frequently like to refer to that experience. Sometimes these references are appropriate and sometimes they are not; you can help them determine when to draw on real-world experiences as evidence or anecdote.
- Adult learners are often very goal oriented, so setting the agenda and successfully wrapping up and summarizing the session are particularly important. Perhaps even more essential, however, is to make sure that the writer leaves with concrete plans for "next steps."
- Do not allow the adult learner to become too dependent on your help. Establish boundaries, and make sure that the writer maintains control over his paper at all times. The strategies for "silence and wait time" outlined in Chapter 2 may be very useful. At the close of the session, the writer may resist leaving and might ask for another session with another tutor immediately. You may need to strongly encourage the writer to work on the draft independently and schedule an appointment for another day.

EXERCISE 4A: Reflecting on Writers' Concerns

Think back over your tutoring sessions, and jot down some responses to the following questions.

- What concerns, besides those relating to their assignment, did writers bring with them?
- How did writers express those concerns?
- How did you respond?

EXERCISE 4B: Reflecting on Your Own Writing Concerns

What concerns have you had over the past year, and how did they affect you as a writer? In what ways can you relate to writers who are multilingual writers, who have writing anxieties, or who have a learning disability? Is English also your second (or third? or fourth?) language, or have you ever tried to learn another language? Have you ever struggled to start an assignment or a task for fear of failure? Have you coped with a learning disability? Have you coped with a disability of another kind—physical or psychological? You might share your thoughts with other tutors and discuss how your experiences influence your role as a writing tutor.

EXERCISE 4C: Reflecting on Tutoring Techniques

Reflect on your experiences tutoring writers who have writing anxieties or learning disabilities or who are multilingual writers, basic writers, or adult learners. Make two lists: one of approaches or techniques that you have found especially useful and a second of those that you have found less helpful. Share your lists with other tutors, and discuss why some techniques were more effective than others.

EXERCISE 4D: Learning from Writers

Interview several writers from one of the identified areas in this chapter. What can you learn from them about their expectations? What works for them when they write? What doesn't work? Ask them to describe a tutoring session that went particularly well and one that did not. What did the tutor do that helped or hindered? What did they wish the tutor had done or had not done?

5

Helping Writers across the Curriculum

Most schools encourage writing across the curriculum—that is, papers are assigned not only in English or writing classes but also in biology, psychology, engineering, and other classes. You will probably tutor writers with assignments from a variety of disciplines, some of which are unfamiliar to you; however, even if you are not an expert on the topic of a paper, you can still help the writer. Tutors often help writers with papers on subjects about which they have no knowledge, such as the benefits of shale for a geology paper or the treatment of knee injuries for a sports-medicine paper. Tutors also help writers with literature papers about works they have never read.

Regardless of a paper's topic, you can determine whether the ideas are presented in a cohesive and persuasive manner. You can look at larger issues—like organization, style, and tone—or at smaller issues—like grammar and mechanics—and determine whether the writing is effective.

It is also helpful to know about conventions for particular kinds of papers, like lab reports or résumés, so that you can ask specific questions to ensure that the assignment is completed effectively. Be aware of various citation styles and distinctions among different fields. If you are unfamiliar with the conventions of the kinds of papers discussed here, check your writing center's print and online resources—writing guides and handbooks, handouts, other information that may be on file, and websites. When possible, use the assignment description as a resource. If questions still arise, suggest that the writer check with the instructor.

RESEARCH PAPERS

The research paper is a common genre in academic writing, and you will undoubtedly tutor many writers with research papers in the writing center. To write an effective one, the writer will need to conduct research, interpret that research, and compose a paper that synthesizes both the writer's and the experts' views of the topic. Proper documentation of evidence is particularly important in research papers; writers may need help selecting appropriate resources to substantiate their claims, integrating information and quotations into their papers, and citing sources within their papers and in their bibliographies.

A CHECKLIST FOR RESEARCH PAPERS

- ❏ If there is a title, is it informative and appropriate?
- ❏ Is the thesis clear? Is the organization logical? If headings and sub-headings are used, do they consistently follow an accepted format?
- ❏ Are sentences varied in length and structure?
- ❏ Are tone, voice, and diction consistent and appropriate?
- ❏ Are transitions smooth from sentence to sentence, paragraph to paragraph, section to section?
- ❏ Are credible sources and evidence used? Is the supporting material suitable and persuasive? Does it adequately support the thesis?
- ❏ Are quotations and paraphrased and summarized passages properly introduced with a signal phrase?
- ❏ Are visual materials — tables, figures, charts, maps, and the like — introduced before they appear in the text?
- ❏ Are long quotations set off from the text?
- ❏ Is proper credit given to sources throughout?
- ❏ Does the paper consistently adhere to the style used (MLA, APA, CMS, CSE, and so on) in format and in documentation, both within the text and in the reference list or list of works cited?
- ❏ Were the instructions for the assignment — length, number and kinds of resources to be used, directions for title page or documentation — followed carefully?

LAB REPORTS AND SCIENTIFIC PAPERS

Lab reports and scientific papers document the results of scientific experimentation and communicate its significance. Typically, lab reports and scientific papers contain the following sections: title page, abstract, introduction, materials and methods, results, discussion, and references. The *title page* includes the name of the experiment, the participating lab partners, and the date; the *abstract* summarizes the purpose, findings, and conclusions of the experiment; the *introduction* contains a statement of objectives and background information; the *materials and methods* provide the list of materials and the procedure (in chronological, narrative format) used for the experiment; the *results* contain the major findings of the study, including calculations and data; the *discussion* includes interpretation and analysis of the data; and the *reference* section lists full citations for all references cited. Lab reports and scientific papers may also contain acknowledgments and appendices.

The major difference between lab reports and scientific papers is that lab reports are shorter documents whose audience is typically a teacher and classmates. A scientific paper contains the same sections as a lab report; however, beyond presenting and interpreting the experiment, it also puts the experiment in conversation with other research in the field and invites further study. Its audience, therefore, is the scientific community at large.

A CHECKLIST FOR LAB REPORTS AND SCIENTIFIC PAPERS

❑ Is the title concise, and does it adequately describe the contents? For example, with the title "Substance Y Alters Blonial Structure of Elephant Bone Marrow," researchers interested in substance Y, blonial structures, elephants, or bone marrow will recognize that the article may be of interest to them.

❑ Are the appropriate headings and subheadings included and in proper order?

❑ Are the tone and style appropriate? Scientific writing, for the most part, is intended to be more factual than entertaining and is not embellished with descriptive language, anecdotes, personal opinion, humor, or dialogue.

❑ Does the writer use passive voice, which is the generally accepted convention? The writer of a lab report, for example, should use the passive past tense: "Solution A was centrifuged," not "I centrifuged Solution A."

❑ Is past tense used for describing the procedures and present tense for describing the results and conclusions?

❑ Are sentences short and to the point, expressing facts clearly and concisely? Does the writer answer all basic questions about the topic?

❑ Have disciplinary conventions related to symbols and abbreviations been observed?

❑ Are figures and tables numbered and accompanied by explanatory captions? Are they introduced before they appear in the text?

ARGUMENT OR POSITION PAPERS

In argument or position papers, writers take stands on debatable issues, such as comprehensive examinations for graduation, required curfews for teenagers, or the causes of global climate changes. Such papers aim to get readers to think differently about a particular issue or to persuade them to take a certain stance. Writers of argument or position papers should envision skeptical audiences and build arguments that are strong enough to stand up to opponents' views. As they write, they should anticipate readers' objections, refuting them or conceding points while indicating, for example, that there are more important issues to be considered.

A CHECKLIST FOR ARGUMENT/POSITION PAPERS

❑ Is the claim or proposition—what the writer is trying to prove—clearly stated?

❑ Are all assertions supported by evidence?

❑ Is the evidence—facts, interpretations of facts, opinions—appropriate? Data should be accurate, recent, and sufficient. Cited sources should be reliable.

❑ Does the arrangement of evidence make sense? Does it emphasize the most important issues? Are there more effective ways of arranging the evidence?

❑ Are facts, statistics, examples, anecdotes, and expert opinions placed properly? Are they used in the appropriate context?

❑ Is the evidence carefully documented?

❑ Is the reasoning sound?

❑ Has the writer avoided all logical fallacies? (If you are unfamiliar with logical fallacies, refer to a writing textbook or handbook or website.)

❑ Are terms that might be controversial or ambiguous adequately defined?

❑ Have opposing arguments been considered and dealt with adequately?

LITERATURE PAPERS

A literature paper analyzes, interprets, or evaluates a text, answering such questions as "What is the significance of the three scaffold scenes in *The Scarlet Letter*?" "What does the cherry orchard in Anton Chekhov's *The Cherry Orchard* represent?" "What is the significance of the setting in John Steinbeck's 'The Chrysanthemums'?" "In *The Plague*, how does Albert Camus' philosophy about social responsibility and the individual's self-interest relate to the Existential movement?" The writer of a literary essay should answer such questions with a meaningful and persuasive analysis that supports ideas and assertions with specific evidence from the text.

A CHECKLIST FOR LITERATURE PAPERS

- ❏ Is the thesis clearly stated? Is the organization logical and easy to follow?
- ❏ Does the writer use examples from the text to convincingly support her interpretation or analysis?
- ❏ Has the writer avoided giving a simple plot summary?
- ❏ Are parts of a work clearly and accurately indicated? Writers need to refer to parts specifically—for example, "the scene in which . . ." or "at the end of Chapter 3."
- ❏ Does the writer use the present tense when describing events in a work of literature, as is the convention? (This practice often confuses writers. You might explain that the author is communicating to a present reader in the present time.)
- ❏ Are titles properly punctuated? Titles of short stories, essays, and most poems appear in quotation marks; titles of books, plays, epics, or other long poems are italicized or underlined.
- ❏ Has the writer referred to the author properly, using the full name initially and the last name in subsequent references?
- ❏ Is quoted material properly punctuated, indented (if longer than four typed lines of prose or three lines of verse), and documented according to the format specified by the teacher?

BOOK, FILM, AND PLAY REVIEWS

Some books, films, or productions of plays are more compelling than others, and reviews describe and evaluate them. Those published in newspapers and other periodicals help readers decide whether they wish to read a book or see a movie or play. They explain what makes a book a "must read" or a movie or film a "must see"; conversely, they describe what makes a work "ho-hum" or a waste of time.

A review does not simply retell what happens. It commonly addresses the purpose, idea, or theme embodied in a work, often in relation to other similar works, and judges its quality by pointing out both strengths and weaknesses. Though reviews cannot deal with every aspect of a work, they should focus on several; for example, a play review might discuss acting, sets, costumes, lighting, and music in addition to the play itself. In reviewing a work, the writer typically describes the criteria of evaluation and offers evidence (quotations, examples, and specific references) to support her opinions. The writer assumes that readers are unfamiliar with the work and thus offers more summary than an analytical piece might, but only enough to create a context for the reader.

A CHECKLIST FOR BOOK, FILM, AND PLAY REVIEWS

❑ Does the first paragraph include the title and other important information, such as the author's, playwright's, or director's name?

❑ Does the introduction give readers an idea of the nature and scope of the work? Does it establish criteria for evaluation?

❑ Are evaluative terms or phrases, such as "good action" or "like a soap opera," defined? (What are the characteristics of good action or soap operas? How does the work embody those characteristics?)

❑ Does an early paragraph orient the reader by briefly summarizing the plot or contents?

❑ Does the review make reasonable assertions and present convincing evidence (quotes, examples, and specific references) to support those assertions?

❑ Is the tone appropriate? Does it suggest that the reviewer is being fair? Does it indicate respect for readers?

❑ Does the reviewer avoid overuse of phrases like "I think" and "in my opinion"? (Such qualifiers may weaken her assertions.)

GROUP WRITING PROJECTS

Teachers sometimes assign a writing project to a group or team. Approaching and completing such a task often overwhelms novice writers, but the instructor should provide most of the information they will need, including procedures the group should follow and what the final product should include.

When you meet with a group, encourage all members to be present. Even if the teacher provides clear directions, a group needs to begin by assuring that everyone understands the guidelines and agrees on how the group will work and what it will produce. Later meetings may continue to focus on the group dynamics, but will also likely consider the document itself and issues like consistency in writing and terminology.

As a tutor, you can help the group to clarify that everyone is working with the same information and has a clear understanding of their process and anticipated outcomes. That typically means that you assume the role of facilitator to help the group decide how to proceed and to clarify and resolve issues that arise. You may listen to the group's concerns, raise questions, facilitate discussions about resolutions, and help the members make plans for further work. You may have to start with posing some basic questions: What are the roles for the members of this group? What has your process been? What will be your process moving toward the deadline? Tell me about communication in your group. How is the writing workflow managed? Simply asking these questions can raise issues for the group to discuss. Often, you can simply interject when needed, but can otherwise let the group resolve the issues.

A common issue is inconsistency among sections written by different students. In fact, a tutoring session may be the first time they've all looked at the paper together. Writers will often notice these problems quickly. You may help the group identify and correct inconsistencies in any of the following areas: grammar, jargon/terminology, data, style, ideas (sections may contradict each other), formatting, and citation.

As you and the group members work with drafts, it can be helpful to use a projector or flat screen, multiple laptops, or paper copies so that everyone can view the paper simultaneously.

A CHECKLIST FOR GROUP WRITING PROJECTS

❑ How has the group structured its work? Is someone "in charge"—at least enough to maintain a schedule of deadlines and coordinate meetings? What specific role does each group member assume? What is each person responsible for? Is there a calendar with deadlines?

❑ What are the teacher's requirements?

❑ What is the purpose of this document? What changes in the reader and his thinking or practices does the group want the paper to effect?

❑ Who is the audience and what are that reader/client's needs? What do they know or need to know? What will they do with the information the group provides?

❑ Are there any broader or secondary audiences? Lay readers? Other professionals in the same or different fields? Legislative assemblies? Bureaucrats? How will the group accommodate them?

❑ How can the information be organized and presented most effectively? Would headings and subheadings, graphics, appendices, or other ways of presenting information be appropriate?

❑ What ancillary information might need to be investigated/presented? How can it be organized/presented most effectively?

❑ What role is the group playing in creating this document? Do they represent students? Concerned citizens? Experts? A combination of roles? How does that role connect to the group's relationship with the audience? What authority do they have? How do they communicate that authority?

DIGITAL OR MULTIMODAL ENVIRONMENTS

Some assignments may ask writers to compose in a digital or multimodal environment, to move from the linear analog model that traditional writing follows to an environment that allows multiple representations of content (text, video, audio, images, interactive elements). As they craft, shape, and present their message, writers can take advantage of the features that various digital platforms and technology provide.

The rapid pace of technological advancements and opportunities and the wide variety of teachers' digital assignments make it difficult to create a comprehensive list of short questions that fit every circumstance. Nonetheless, a tutor can work with a writer to answer these broad questions. Encourage writers to take more specific questions back to their teachers.

- ❑ Does the writer purposefully, thoughtfully, and effectively make use of available features so that they add depth to the message and reach the audience?
- ❑ Has the writer carefully considered how a reader might read the digital text in its digital environment? Although print texts typically are read top to bottom, digital texts often have multiple pages, with options to hyperlink in and out of the text. Consequently, the writer may need to consider additional organizational strategies.
- ❑ Does the writer consider the appropriateness of choices like images, graphics, color, font, and the like for her established audience and purpose?
- ❑ Are there any potential issues of accessibility? Will the multimodal text work via multiple browsers, at various bandwidths, and so forth?
- ❑ If appropriate or necessary, has the writer secured permission from the participants to be featured in her presentation (photographed, videographed, or otherwise)?

POWERPOINT AND ALTERNATIVE PLATFORM PRESENTATIONS

One digital platform that has stood the test of time and continues to be popular for writers is PowerPoint. Many writers use PowerPoint for multimedia presentations, and you may encounter writers who need help creating and refining these presentations. A PowerPoint presentation facilitates an oral presentation that gives information, explores research, teaches concepts, or proposes a course of action. It offers visual guidelines that outline information as well as reinforce key terms and concepts. These guidelines may include pictures, video clips, or other visual aids that illustrate or highlight points made in the presentation.

Because templates make it easy to create PowerPoint presentations, some writers do so without carefully considering their audience, purpose, or ethos (their credibility or authority in the eyes of the audience). They may crowd each slide with information, expecting it to *be* the presentation rather than to facilitate it. Or, they may get carried away and load the presentation with visuals, so that the audience pays more attention to the glitz than to the presenter's ideas.

Alternative platforms like Prezi, PowToon, and GoAnimate also offer templates for presenting information using slides, voiceover, or animation with varying degrees of interaction and sophistication. In addition to items in the checklist below, there may be other considerations to determine the presentation's effectiveness that depend upon the particular platform. Regardless of your familiarity with these platforms, you can always respond as a potential viewer and explain what about the presentation seems more or less effective.

A CHECKLIST FOR POWERPOINT AND ALTERNATIVE PLATFORM PRESENTATIONS

❑ Has the writer carefully considered the audience, purpose, and occasion for the presentation?

❑ Has the writer carefully considered his position in relation to the audience and how he wishes to be perceived by them (ethos)?

❑ Does the presentation truly complement the talk? Is the amount of text on each slide appropriate?

❑ Is the slide progression logical? Is the text simple and phrased in a consistent manner (parallelism)?

❑ If appropriate, does the presentation reinforce key concepts or phrases?

❑ Do the text, images, tables, graphs, and other visual aids facilitate and complement the presentation? Can they be seen clearly from a distance?

❑ Does white space appropriately set off text, images, tables, graphs, and other visual aids?

❑ Are the colors, fonts, background, and themes appropriate and consistent?

RÉSUMÉS (TRADITIONAL)

The résumé and cover letter are designed to get a job interview, not to secure a job, as some writers believe. The résumé simply offers a prospective employer a quick look at an applicant's educational and work history and provides

"VERY impressive resume, Mr. Miller!"

other pertinent information, such as special skills, awards, and interests. It also serves as a marketing tool for the applicant, highlighting relevant skills and successful work and education experiences and achievements. Nonetheless, it should be succinct and clear so that prospective employers can absorb information at a glance. (Keep in mind that the résumé you are helping with may be one of hundreds that an employer has to read; each résumé typically gets 30 seconds of attention.)

Be aware that résumé practices change over time and know the most recent ones. After five years, for example, many people omit graduation dates. Some also omit addresses, assuming that contact typically occurs via telephone or e-mail. If in doubt as to how to advise a writer, consider the position and audience for the résumé; include the address if applying for a more conservative position or if there is any question about whether to include it. Note, too, that references are not usually listed unless requested, nor is the statement "References will be furnished upon request" included. As for fonts, debate continues between using the cleaner sans-serif fonts, like Arial, or serif fonts with their decorative flourishes on letters and symbols, like Times New

Roman. Given a choice, opt for the former as some consider it more modern. Use at least a size-10 font to assure readability and use formatting like bold-face and underlining judiciously.

Content on a résumé is generally listed in reverse chronological order; however, in terms of listing work and education, there's no rule for what comes first. Recent graduates typically list education first, but it depends on what the applicant wishes to emphasize. Those with lots of experience may wish to promote work history. While composing their résumés, writers often downplay work experience that they think is irrelevant to the job that they are seeking. They assume, for example, that being a bartender or server in a restaurant has little or no relevance to a marketing position. What they do not realize is that the personnel manager of a marketing firm might be impressed by the fact that an applicant spent three years with the same res-taurant, won the Employee of the Month award, or had responsibilities for handling money or training new employees. Writers should consider how seemingly irrelevant experience might relate to certain aspects of a particular job or demonstrate qualities of a desirable applicant and highlight those con-nections in their résumés and cover letters.

A CHECKLIST FOR RÉSUMÉS

❏ Is the résumé pleasing to the eye? Held up at a distance, it should appear visually balanced, not crowded at the top or off to one side.

❏ Is all necessary information included? Check for the writer's name, address, telephone number(s), and e-mail address. Review and ask questions about education, professional or related experience, and other experience.

❏ Is the e-mail address appropriate for a prospective employer? It should contain the applicant's name and not be cavalier or suggestive. (Certainly muscleman@xyz.com is inappropriate, but references to political or religious groups and even sports teams or hobbies are best not used when applying for a job.) You might also remind writers to be sure their voice-mail messages and public social media accounts are appropriately professional.

❏ Has the writer eliminated all unnecessary information (such as gender, marital status, number of children, or political or religious affiliation)?

❏ Are the parts logically and effectively arranged?

❏ Is the length appropriate? Unless there is a good reason, a résumé should generally be no longer than one page and certainly no longer than two pages.

❏ If an objective is included, is it accurate? (As a professional or career objective, students sometimes write that they seek "an entry-level posi-tion as a . . . ," but an entry-level position is an immediate objective, not a long-term goal. Applicants should focus on how the job fits into their career goals, not just their short-term job goals.)

☐ If a summary statement is included, would it catch the prospective employer's eye and answer the question, "What can this person do for me/my company?" Does it succinctly showcase qualifications, strengths, and accomplishments, highlighting specific areas of expertise and the applicant's commitment to them?

☐ Are education and work history (and other such information) in reverse chronological order, with most recent activities listed first?

☐ Has the writer considered all relevant experience, such as volunteer work, internships, coursework, and school projects?

☐ Are job descriptions unnecessarily wordy? (For example, phrases like "responsible for" can often be omitted or tightened.) Furthermore, has the writer emphasized his strengths without exaggerating or misleading the reader?

☐ Are all items in lists in parallel grammatical form? (For example, the list "writing proposals, trained new employees, planned staff meetings, Employee of the Year" is not parallel. A parallel version is "wrote proposals, trained new employees, planned staff meetings, earned Employee of the Year award.")

☐ Is the résumé error free? Misspellings, grammatical mistakes, and other errors may cause employers to ask, "If this person is careless in writing a résumé, what kind of work can I expect from her?" Note that sending a document as a pdf eliminates the chance that formatting may change as a document is transmitted.

RÉSUMÉS (SCANNABLE)

To sort through and store numbers of résumés, many employers use optical character recognition (OCR) technology, which searches for keywords. These words are nouns and sometimes adjectives that describe specific skills. While some are general—like *leadership*, *communication*, or *entrepreneurial*—most are specific to particular occupations, industries, and positions. For example, a list of keywords for a position as a social worker might contain *clinical experience*, *family services*, *crisis intervention*, and *LCSW*. For an accountant, the list could include terms like *CPA*, *G/L experience*, *public accounting*, and names of specific computer accounting programs. Keywords should be incorporated throughout the résumé and punctuation should be avoided as much as possible; the computer might not recognize a keyword if a comma or period immediately follows it. A keyword summary may also be placed at the end of the résumé.

A CHECKLIST FOR SCANNABLE RÉSUMÉS

❑ Do keywords define education, experience, and skills? Has the writer effectively turned verbs into nouns when appropriate—for example, *designing* into *design specialist* or *coordinating* into *project coordinator?*

❑ Has the writer used common abbreviations, acronyms, and jargon specific to the field, like *BA* for *bachelor of arts*, or *CAD* for *computer-assisted design?*

❑ Is the résumé left-justified on standard-sized paper?

❑ Is the font a standard typeface? Is the size 10 or 12 points?

❑ Has punctuation been avoided as much as possible?

❑ Is there white space between words and letters (letters must not touch one another)?

❑ Has the writer avoided using italics, underlining, and special characters like bullets?

❑ Has the writer avoided using graphics, shading, boxes, and horizontal and vertical lines?

❑ If the résumé content must be pasted into text boxes instead of uploaded, has the writer double-checked for any resulting formatting issues?

COVER LETTERS

Writers should know that, unless otherwise indicated, a résumé must always be accompanied by a cover letter. In these letters, applicants should clearly indicate the position being sought, mention how they learned about it (on an online job board, through another person, and so on), and explain how their qualifications suit each requirement listed in the job description. Finally, they should request an interview.

A CHECKLIST FOR COVER LETTERS

❑ Does the letter follow an acceptable format for a business letter? (See a website or a handbook for a discussion of business-letter formats.)

❑ Is the letter addressed to a person rather than to a position? ("Dear Ms. Plotnic" is preferable to "Dear Personnel Manager.") Consider checking the company website or making a telephone call to get this information.

❑ Does the first paragraph specifically identify the position being sought?

❑ Does the letter indicate how the applicant learned about the position?

❑ Does the letter acknowledge all requirements mentioned in the ad or job description?

❏ Does the applicant talk in terms of what he can do for the employer rather than the other way around? (With the exception of those applying for internships, which are set up to help people learn and gain hands-on experience, applicants are assumed to bring knowledge or expertise to a position; therefore, statements like "I expect to increase my knowledge about the accounting field" are out of place.)

❏ Is the letter error free?

APPLICATION ESSAYS AND PERSONAL STATEMENTS

Writers often ask for help with essays of application for undergraduate or graduate programs as well as other programs. Writers sometimes have difficulty envisioning the audience for their essay, so asking them to describe their readers can be a good place to start. Writers may not realize that readers will likely be professional people, but their expertise may not lie in the applicant's area of interest. Someone with degrees and experience in electrical or aerospace engineering, for example, may weigh in on an application for graduate school in mechanical engineering. At the same time, these readers are

**The bane of every college applicant:
the admissions essay.**

people with personal, political, and cultural sensitivities. They also probably have many essays to read in a short amount of time. Articulating the readers' characteristics should help the writer make more thoughtful decisions as he composes his essay.

Though you will need to consider the usual aspects of an essay—like content, organization, tone, and grammar—you need to keep a number of other specific points in mind with essays of application.

A CHECKLIST FOR APPLICATION ESSAYS

❏ Does the writer establish the point of the essay early on? Instead of including many themes, does she focus on one or two that allow her to go deeper rather than be superficial? Is the relevance of the information clearly established? Avoid the mistake made by one applicant, who wrote a lengthy essay describing her harrowing escape from her homeland. Though her point was that if she could withstand those rigors she could manage medical school, she confused readers by waiting until the end to tell them her reason for relating her story.

❏ Does the introduction engage the reader? Does it avoid trite statements like "Ever since I was four and put bandages on my doll, I have wanted to be a doctor"? How will this essay fare against the many others that are being read? A note of caution: Readers want to see how an applicant differs from other applicants, but they can quickly spot outrageous or excessive statements. The writer needs to consider the readers of the application—who they are and what they might be looking for.

❏ On a related point, does the essay sound sincere and honest, or has the writer exaggerated? (For example, becoming a teacher to "change the world" is clearly beyond one person's capabilities.)

❏ Has the writer completely answered the question being posed? Some applications simply ask why one has chosen a particular career or program. Others ask applicants to discuss their strengths and weaknesses, ethics, work experience, accomplishments, or extracurricular activities.

❏ Has the writer included sufficient evidence—often anecdotal—with details that show rather than tell? (For example, rather than write "I am a community-minded person," the applicant should describe what he has accomplished that demonstrates that attitude.)

❏ Has the writer appropriately eliminated extraneous details that do not contribute anything to the essay? (For example, Aunt Mary's illness may have led the writer to consider becoming a doctor. Unless there is good reason, however, readers do not need to know what Aunt Mary prefers for breakfast or the kind of car she drives.)

❏ Does the writer use positive statements and subordination to downplay negative points? A student who received Bs while studying abroad deftly demonstrated this tactic on a law school application by explaining, "When I studied in Spain, I took all courses in Spanish, knowing that doing so would significantly improve my facility with the language, but also likely lower my grade-point average."

❑ Is the essay error free? Misspellings, grammatical errors, and other mechanical problems may cause readers to question an applicant's attention to detail.

6

Tutoring in the Information Age

Writing centers today enjoy having a great variety of social media and technological tools at their disposal. Many writing centers offer online tutoring, use various social media accounts, and maintain blogs or web pages of writing resources. Moreover, online search engines are students' go-to resources for initial research for essays, and the distinction between print and online resources is diminishing rapidly. But this ease of access and plethora of information comes at a cost: online tutors are faced with an array of online platforms and tools, each with its own learning curve and quirks; similarly, writers are faced with research topics that generate thousands of hits on an online search engine and are often overwhelmed and confused with how to appropriately vet and cite these sources. Whether you tutor online for your writing center, contribute to your writing center's social media, or help students face-to-face with questions about the validity of online research sources, this chapter will address the special considerations of tutoring in the information age.

For further information, we suggest you consult the collection of resources compiled and developed through the National Council of Teachers of English (NCTE) Committee for Effective Practices in Online Writing Instruction: www.ncte.org/cccc/committees/owi. Here you can find an Open Resource collection, surveys, best practices position statements, and an annotated bibliography that includes a writing center section.

ONLINE TUTORING

Online tutoring appeals to writers for a variety of reasons. Students now expect various components of their college experience to be digital: they register for classes online, renew their library books online, and text their friends

and family between classes. As the number of nontraditional students on campuses grows, nontraditional methods of learning and teaching increase as well. Time and distance no longer restrict learning to a classroom, as students can attend classes virtually. Writers can also often access the writing center from a remote site, which makes tutorial assistance available to many who might otherwise be unable to take advantage of it. From home, work, dorm room, or local coffee shop, writers can access writing center resources, chat with a tutor, or submit their papers electronically for feedback.

In general, there are two kinds of online communication: *synchronous* and *asynchronous*. Synchronous online communication happens in real time: online at the same time, two or more people can text chat, collaborate on a document, and/or video conference. Asynchronous online communication, like e-mail, happens outside of real time, with minutes, hours, or days between correspondences. Below are a few of the more common forms of synchronous and asynchronous tutoring.

Synchronous Tutoring

- **Chat via instant messaging:** Tutor and writer log on at the same time and confer online.

- **Internet phone:** Tutor calls the writer using free Internet phone, such as Skype, and the two discuss the paper.
- **Web conferencing:** Tutor and writer log on to a web-based conferencing platform and chat and work online, sometimes with a webcam. Many of these are free apps, web-based services that include such features as document sharing, whiteboard space, chat boxes, and calendars. If the writer shares his document, the tutor and writer can work synchronously, using such features as highlighting, underlining, or commenting to move through the paper together. If the writer doesn't yet have a document to share, then the tutor and writer can use the virtual blank slate of whiteboard space to just draw and chat, perhaps exploring the writer's ideas by sketching a clustered diagram or jotting down brainstorming ideas.
- **Social media:** Tutor signs into and manages a social media account, posting resources, sending reminders for workshops, and updating pictures and news. Some writing centers use social media messaging applications for quick questions that may not require a full tutoring session.

Asynchronous Tutoring

- **E-mail:** Writer e-mails her paper to the writing center. Tutors are forwarded papers from a central e-mail server, or they check a shared e-mail account at appointed times.
- **Database:** Writer submits a paper to an online database. A coordinator or supervisor assigns papers as they come in, and tutors log on to the system and retrieve the papers from an inbox. After the tutor finishes reviewing the paper, he uploads his advice to the database, and it is then forwarded to the writer.
- **Online classroom:** Tutor facilitates a writing workshop in an online classroom. There may be chat features available, but the majority of conversation is threaded: that is, the writer asks a question and the tutor responds, or the tutor posts a topic and discussion question and the writer responds, and so on.

Throughout the other chapters of this book, we have included examples of synchronous tutoring. Indeed, because of the commonplace availability of excellent real time platforms and applications, strategies and considerations for in-person tutoring translate quite seamlessly into synchronous online tutoring. A tutor can ask a question; a writer can immediately respond. A writer can compose a thesis statement; a tutor can immediately comment on it. And online environments often have drawing and reviewing features that can help the tutor accommodate a range of learning styles.

For a variety of reasons, like access issues and scheduling considerations, some writing centers choose to use asynchronous tutoring as their primary online medium. At first consideration, you may think that synchronous online tutoring is always preferable because it most closely resembles face-to-face tutoring. However, let's look at four significant advantages of asynchronous online tutoring.

- **Time.** For many tutors and writers, the biggest difference between synchronous and asynchronous online tutoring is the time factor. With in-person and synchronous tutoring, writers get immediate feedback. With asynchronous tutoring, however, they must often allow for a turnaround time that can range from a few hours to several days, depending on the writing center's policies and the way incoming papers are monitored. However, this additional time gives the asynchronous tutor more flexibility and means that he can potentially go into greater depth with feedback and refine advice. Furthermore, it gives the writer an opportunity to step away from the assignment, then return to it with a fresh and potentially new perspective. For especially challenging papers, the tutor can take a break and approach the paper refreshed or take the time to ask another tutor for help.

- **Collaboration.** Many of you may be nervous about losing the collaborative quality of in-person and synchronous tutoring. In asynchronous environments, both tutors and writers may initially miss the physical proximity and immediate rapport that conversation provides, but as you work together you will build a written rapport and may very well come to feel like pen pals. You may also access the writer's previous submissions and advice and refer to them in your comments, thus contributing to an ongoing conversation about her writing.

- **Anonymity.** Because the tutor and writer cannot see each other, the potential intrusion of some stereotypes diminishes. Gender, race, and class become more ambiguous, and shy or socially anxious tutors and writers may feel less inhibited in an online environment.

- **Written record.** While the lack of verbal exchange can have disadvantages, writers may gain from having a written copy of a tutor's suggestions. For multilingual learners, in particular, a face-to-face session can be confusing if a tutor uses idioms or talks quickly; written comments may be more useful because the writer can read them over and over for better understanding or, if necessary, take time to translate them. Writers can digitally save their asynchronous written advice for later retrieval and use.

Because asynchronous tutoring requires a unique set of strategies, the remainder of this section will provide tools for conducting successful asynchronous online tutoring sessions. The asynchronous tutoring session begins much like the face-to-face or synchronous tutoring session, with the writer telling the tutor about the assignment and the specific concerns that she has regarding the paper. When writers send papers electronically, they generally identify the course and the assignment and explain what they would like the tutor to concentrate on as he reads.

However, in an asynchronous session tutors cannot use certain signals—like body language and tone of voice—to gauge the writer's level of understanding and the session's progress in order to make decisions about how to proceed. Nor can they simply ask the writer clarifying questions and get immediate feedback, as they might if conferring face-to-face or through synchronous chat. Occasionally, this lack of signals may lead to confusion on the part of tutor or writer, a problem that can be resolved by taking the time to e-mail the writer with brief questions to settle any issues before continuing with the paper. Likewise, writers can use e-mail or chat to request clarification if they have any questions after reading the tutor's responses.

Asynchronous feedback on a paper should be similar to feedback that you would give in a face-to-face tutorial. Ask questions frequently, and offer statements to indicate that you are responding as a reader. If it is helpful, use a standard form or template created by you or in collaboration with other tutors. A standard template can frame your response to the student as well as ensure a certain consistency in approach and focus. Be sure that your template covers both big picture and sentence-level concerns and allows you to respond to a range of writing issues, from working on the thesis to identifying and correcting comma splices. For an example, see the University of Maryland University College's Effective Writing Center's advice template on page 100.

Just as in face-to-face sessions, the tutor's ultimate focus should remain on helping the student to become a better writer rather than on simply making the piece of writing more effective. Here are some general suggestions for successful online tutoring, followed by specific advice for conducting an asynchronous online tutoring session.

SOME SUGGESTIONS FOR ASYNCHRONOUS ONLINE TUTORING

- Check e-mail or log on to chat areas at regular intervals so that writers are attended to and papers are assigned in a timely manner.
- Maintain communication, both with other writing center staff and with writers. Keep your online supervisor or coordinator informed of schedule changes or technological conflicts so that he can inform the writer if there will be a delay. If you—the tutor—are the primary point of contact for the writer, keep the writer informed. E-mail the writer to say that you have received the paper and will be in touch soon. If a situation changes, communicate with the writer immediately: "I've been called out of town, but I've given your paper to Yao. You'll be hearing from him this afternoon." Reassurance is important, especially to apprehensive writers.
- Read through the paper completely before making any comments, and think about how the paper works as a whole. As you read, be mindful

of any specific questions that the writer may have included with his online submission or e-mail and consider whether the paper fulfills the assignment.

- If you have access to other technologies, such as audio software, consider embedding audio comments in your advice as well. Audio comments, although still asynchronous, often seem more personal to the writer and appeal to auditory learners.

- Just as in face-to-face tutoring, use your initial comments to establish rapport and make the writer feel comfortable. Introduce yourself with relevant details, such as your background and the length of time you have been tutoring.

- When you identify problematic areas in the paper, always provide examples from the writer's paper as well as an example or a model of a possible resolution. Be specific. Rather than "You need to strengthen your evidence for your second point," write, "I was a bit confused after reading your fifth through seventh paragraphs. You make the following claim, '[quotation from paper],' but I don't see how you back up that claim. Do you have some research that will support this?"

- Resist the urge to simply edit. For new online tutors working directly with a text, this tendency can be strong. Use editing tools cautiously and sparingly and be careful that you do not fall into the trap of editing for the writer. Your purpose is not to proofread, and simply editing the paper actually does the writer a disservice because she will not know what to do differently next time. Instead, point out recurring errors, and explain the relevant writing rules. It is more effective to look for significant patterns of writing issues than to simply start at the beginning, marking each "problem" as you read; you can then comment on the patterns you see and the ways to fix or avoid them. As a way of modeling, some tutors edit a small portion of the text with explanations for each change and then suggest that the writer go through the rest of the paper and make similar corrections.

- Consider carefully if you will use embedded comments (track changes) or a template letter or form. Remember that directly marking the writer's paper could be misinterpreted by faculty as plagiarism. It can also suggest to students that only the places you've marked need to be corrected and that they need not look at the rest of their text. Moreover, instead of carefully considering advice and making revisions on their own, the act of simply "accepting changes" in track changes is antithetical to writing center best practices. For this reason, some online centers do not allow embedded comments; they limit tutors' feedback to comments at the beginning or end of the paper.

- Use humor and sarcasm carefully. These don't translate as well in writing as they do face-to-face and can offend writers inadvertently.

- If you have access to the writer's earlier sessions through e-mails or submissions and advice, refer to them. These reminders will prompt the writer to take another look at previous comments and will reinforce what you or another tutor advised earlier.
- Write an encouraging closing note. Praise what is done well and explain why it is effective, but do not be too effusive. Your comments should be genuine but still acknowledge that there is work to be done. Remind the writer that the paper is a draft by using phrases such as "For a draft, your paper ..." Be careful with statements such as "This is a great paper," as the writer can easily misinterpret it to mean "You'll get an A."
- Watch your time. If your writing center has established time limits for each online session, adhere to them. Generally, you will want to finish tutoring a paper within one sitting. Try not to take too many or lengthy breaks; they may interrupt your concentration on the paper and make giving advice more difficult.

STOCK ONLINE RESPONSES. Stock responses are explanations that you compose ahead of time for questions and concepts that come up often, such as "writing a thesis," "effective sentence combining," or "integrating quotations." Written by you or cowritten with other tutors, these stock responses will save you time. However, keep in mind that you should always personalize stock responses to the writer's specific and individual concerns. Remember to revise your repertoire of stock responses as you become more familiar and more comfortable with various writing concepts.

The following is an example of stock advice for constructing paragraphs from the University of Maryland University College's Effective Writing Center. Note how the tutor identifies the writing issue, provides a description along with a generic example, applies the stock advice to the writer's specific example, and finally links to additional resources.

STOCK RESPONSE FOR CONSTRUCTING PARAGRAPHS

How can I develop strong paragraphs? What do I need to include? — Tutor identifies the issue.

✓ Smooth topic sentences with smooth transitional tone.
✓ Body information supporting the topic sentence.

The first sentence in a new paragraph is a topic sentence. This sentence should accomplish two things: It should introduce the new topic and do so with a smooth tone. Adding transition words and rearranging word order can help accomplish this. Here is an example of a smooth topic sentence: "Because of the many roles a working parent has, the first priority includes planning out an organized daily schedule." Do you see how starting with the transition word **because** helped create a smooth topic sentence? The last sentence of a paragraph should wrap up the main idea before you move on to the next paragraph. — Tutor provides a description and generic example.

Jeremy, your paragraphs are filled with so much good informa-
tion, but there are times when I am not sure what point you are
making. Are you concentrating on the fact that cell phone use is
dangerous while driving? Is it that letting your kids distract you
is the dangerous thing while driving? Is it that education is the
key to learning how to drive safely? I am not certain where your
essay is going because you never provided that definite and clear
thesis statement. That thesis statement is so important to your
essay as a whole. All body paragraphs should support the thesis
statement. You will want to keep this in mind as you revise and
get your paragraphs to match your thesis.

— Tutor applies stock advice to the writer's specific example.

If you have more questions on paragraphs or transitions, please take advantage of this UMUC audio advice:

— Tutor links to additional resources.

UMUC Audio Tutorials: Paragraphs (http://polaris.umuc.edu
/ewc/tutorials/paragraphs/)
UMUC Audio Tutorials: Transitions (http://polaris.umuc.edu
/ewc/tutorials/transitions/)

ONLINE WRITING RESOURCES

In addition to offering almost limitless opportunities for research, the Internet provides access to writing resources both for you and for the writers you tutor. These resources are especially convenient if you are tutoring online; however, they can also be valuable in face-to-face tutoring. Your center may also have writing tutorial software for writers to use individually or with your assistance; in face-to-face situations it may sometimes be appropriate to leave writers at the computer to do research, use a tutorial, or compose on their own. While we cannot list all the resources available online, we can offer explanations of the kinds of resources and indicate important points to consider when you work with writers or use these resources yourself. The following is a partial list of online writing resources.

Online Writing Labs

Many writing centers have established online writing labs, or OWLs, that offer information about their services, staff, and location as well as access to worksheets, style manuals, and research tools. Many also take advantage of the Web's ability to link to documents at other sites, thus increasing the amount of available material. You can easily find another writing center's OWL by going to the college or university's main web page and doing a search for *writing center* or *writing lab*.

Online Writing Guides and Handbooks

Online writing guides and handbooks differ from OWLs in that OWLs are a compilation of resources, and online writing guides offer a single, comprehensive resource. Typically, online writing guides are more linear in format; many even have chapters. They may offer a variety of online resources, including interactive writing exercises, grammar exercises, research exercises, and model papers.

Online Videos

Many writing centers develop and post videos online to augment training and to share writing resources. Online tutor-training videos provide a full sense of the tutorial, including both nonverbal and verbal communication, and offer examples of a variety of types of tutoring. Many writing centers also create and share online videos on a variety of writing issues.

HELPING WRITERS EVALUATE ONLINE SOURCES

In addition to tutoring having a place online, researching and writing have evolved into processes that are often conducted there as well. Most print resources, such as journals and books, go through a review or filtering process, like editing or peer review (a draft of this book, for example, was read by several people who offered comments and suggestions for revision). Information on the Internet, however, is sometimes unfiltered. In essence, the Web can be a kind of vanity press; almost anyone can publish on it, and some resources are not verified by traditional publishers, editors, or reviewers.

Sometimes, a writer will express confusion over how to find and cite credible web resources. In such cases, consider modeling online research for him. As a tutor, it is important that you know the criteria for evaluating information found on the Web as you help guide writers conducting online research for their assignments.

The three main elements of a web document are its header, its body, and its footer (see the example "Web Page Elements" on the facing page). By looking at these components, you should be able to determine the following information, which can then be used to evaluate the document:

- Author or contact person (usually found in the footer)
- Institution, organization, or company (usually found in either the header or footer)
- Date of creation or last revision (usually found in the footer)
- Intended audience (determined by examining the body)

- Intended purpose of the document (determined by examining the body)
- Link to local home page (usually found in the header or footer)

Writers need to consider the authority, accuracy, bias, and currency of any information—whether in print, on film, or online. What follows are some suggestions for helping writers to determine these criteria when they use Internet sources.

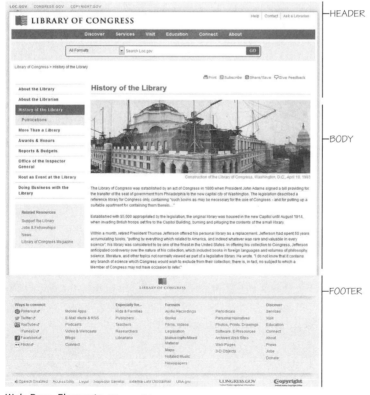

Web Page Elements. Library of Congress.

Authority

With any material, you need to determine both the author of the text and the basis of authority from which the author speaks. Because anyone can publish on the Web, it is sometimes difficult to determine authorship of a document, and frequently a person's qualifications for speaking on a topic are absent or questionable. If you do not recognize the author as being well-known and respected in the field, here are some possible ways to determine authority:

- Did you find the address for or link to the author's document from another reliable document?
- Does the document give substantive biographical information about the author so that you can evaluate his or her credentials, or can you get this information by following a link to another document?
- Is the author referenced or mentioned positively by another author or organization whose authority you trust?

If the publisher or sponsor is an organization, you may generally assume that the document meets the standards and aims of the group. You may want to consider the following:

- Is this organization suitable to address this topic?
- Is this organization recognized and respected in the field?
- What relationship does the author have to the publisher or sponsor— does the document tell you something about the author's expertise or qualifications?

Accuracy

You may be reading information presented by an author or organization unfamiliar to you and need to verify accuracy. Criteria for evaluating accuracy might include the following:

- Are the sources that the document relies on linked or included in a bibliography?
- Is the background information verified? If not, can it be verified?
- Is the methodology appropriate for the topic?
- If the online document is a research project, does the data that was gathered include explanations of research methods and interpretations?
- Is the site modified or updated regularly?

Bias

To determine bias, remember that any responsible author situates her work within a context. Since this context reveals what an author knows about the subject as well as her stance on the topic, check the following:

- Was the site developed by a recognized academic institution, government agency, or national, international, or commercial organization with an established reputation in the subject area?
- Does the author show knowledge of theories, techniques, or schools of thought that usually are related to the topic?
- Does the author show knowledge of related sources and attribute them properly?
- Does the author discuss the value and limitations of the approach if it is new?
- Does the author acknowledge that the subject matter itself or her treatment of it is controversial if you know that to be the case?

Currency

Information on some subjects will change rapidly, while for others, it may not change at all. For historical topics like the Industrial Revolution, older articles may still be quite useful and valuable. For more contemporary topics related to science or technology, however, currency may be extremely important. You will need to consider the following when examining the document:

- Does it mention dates of publication, most recent update, or copyright?
- Does it give dates showing when information was gathered?
- Does it give information about new material when appropriate?

EXERCISE 6A: The Challenges of Online Tutoring

Consider an activity that you used to perform mostly face-to-face but that you now do online, like shopping, banking, library research, or gaming. Think about mediums of communication, like phone calls and letters, that are now frequently conducted online. What has been lost and/or gained in this transition?

As a student, have you taken courses both face-to-face and online? If so, what were the significant differences? What were the advantages and disadvantages of each approach? Which did you prefer and why?

Bearing in mind your answers to the questions above, what do you think are the unique challenges and opportunities of online tutoring?

EXERCISE 6B: Creating Stock Responses

Identify three or four writing issues that you often encounter as you work with writers. Try to think of both global and sentence-level issues; then write stock responses for each of these issues. For an example, see the stock response for constructing paragraphs on pages 94–95 of this chapter.

EXERCISE 6C: Developing Advice Templates

Review the standardized template below. What are its strengths? What are its weaknesses? By yourself or working with other tutors in your writing center, develop an advice template for your writing center. Try it out in a peer review session in class, or make arrangements to use it reviewing a writer's paper.

STANDARDIZED TEMPLATE. Tutors at the University of Maryland University College's completely online writing center use a standardized template when replying to student drafts. The template is structured so that larger elements (content, organization, and paragraph skills) are treated before sentence-level concerns. We provide our modified version of their template below, with descriptions of each section. Throughout the session the tutor more or less follows this strategy: (1) identify a writing issue or two; (2) define that issue; (3) copy and paste a representative portion from the writer's paper into the template; (4) offer feedback, sometimes by modeling a correction; and (5) provide links to other online resources. When appropriate, the tutor embeds audio and/or video comments and resources as well.

Date _____

Dear [writer's name],

Congratulations on your progress in writing this assignment for [class]. [Tutors should feel free to add compliments, encouragement, or other personal statements to establish warmth and connection. It's helpful to compliment a specific **writing-related skill or strength**, and then explain **why** it is a strength, for example, "This is what you did well, and this is why it is good."]

My name is [so and so], and it's my pleasure to work with you today. [Tutors can insert avatar, video, or audio greetings here.]

> **SALUTATION**
> In addition to greeting the writer by name to establish connection and rapport, tutors also use this opening section to offer compliments and encouragement, setting a positive and supportive tone from the very beginning. Tutors may include a video welcome message that is also transcribed into the advice.

You are welcome to come to the Effective Writing Center for help at any stage in the writing process, whether you are having trouble understanding an assignment or want feedback on a rough draft. At the EWC we are attentive readers who help you improve as a writer by explaining and modeling effective writing skills. For a more detailed discussion of our services, please visit the Effective Writing Center website.

The Effective Writing Center also offers live, one-on-one online advising via teleconference. [Tutors are free to include thumbnails or other links here, according to preference.]

> **ADVICE OVERVIEW**
> This section explains writing center policies and procedures. The tutor can also alert the student to what areas of the paper will receive special attention and can provide information on any unique features of his advice template. For example, the tutor may explain how he uses a system of color-coding (student's text in one color and the tutor's in another, etc.) or hyperlinking within the advice letter.

Please note:

- Tutors may not be experts in the topic your paper covers.

- Tutors will not make any judgment about the grade your paper may receive.

- Tutors do not copyedit papers. Sections of your paper will be used to model the editing you should do.

- Tutors know only as much about the assignment as you share. Please provide an assignment description on the submission form.

Resources to help you revise your writing assignment are hyperlinked within this letter and in the More Resources section at the end. Before reading this advice, please review the writing that you submitted and have a copy handy.

Assignment Requirement	You Have	You Need

ASSIGNMENT REQUIREMENTS
Here the tutor compares the assignment requirements to what the writer has submitted.
Some tutors use a table in this section that lists: (1) each assignment requirement; (2) what the writer has provided for that requirement; (3) what is needed, if anything, to fulfill the requirements. The tutor reads through the paper first before addressing this section.

Thesis & Organization

[Tutors comment on the overall focus and arrangement, including introductory and concluding paragraphs and the use of headings. This section may include the following topics: thesis statement, organization/outlining, transitions, cohesion, and introductions and conclusions.]

Development & Research

[Tutors comment on the use of supportive material in the essay, specifically on development, unity, and coherence. This section may include the following topics: paragraph development, length, structure, and unity, and research development and incorporation.]

Formatting & Citations

[Tutors comment on manuscript formatting, documentation, and the paper's adherence to the student's chosen or assigned style (APA, MLA, Chicago, Turabian, Blue Book, AAA, etc.).]

Grammar & Mechanics

[Tutors comment on grammar, punctuation, and other sentence-level revisions and concerns.]

BODY OF ADVICE LETTER
The body of the advice letter contains four main sections. All explanations within these sections include specific reference to the student's paper (i.e., a description of what's in the paper or excerpts that are copied and pasted from the paper); explanations, models, and strategies to aid in revision; and a hyperlink to a resource where the student can learn more.

I enjoyed reading your paper and learning more about [topic].
I particularly found [offer at least one item of positive feed-
back]. Good luck as you finish this paper! As you continue
your work on this project, be sure to:

1.

2.

3.

4.

SUMMARY
*Tutors provide num-
bered list of action
items for the writer;
this list summarizes
the tutor's suggestions
for improvement.*

[*Your Name*]
The Effective Writing Center
www.umuc.edu/ewc
University of Maryland University College
3501 University Boulevard East, Adelphi, Maryland 20783

TUTOR INFO
*Tutors list only their
names and the contact
information for the
writing center. They do
not list any personal
contact information.*

- UMUC Effective Writing Center
  http://www.umuc.edu/writingcenter/index.cfm
- hyperlink to resource
- hyperlink to resource
- hyperlink to resource

RESOURCES
*Tutors list the URLs
of the links provided
throughout the tem-
plate in addition to the
writing center's website
and any additional
resources.*

7

Addressing Various Tutoring Situations

Writers do not bring just their papers to the writing center; they often also bring anxieties, stress, and other personal issues. Thus, you will occasionally encounter some troublesome—or perhaps even difficult—situations while tutoring. A writer who has writing anxiety may come at the last minute, desperate for help. Or, a writer may come only at the insistence of a teacher and be difficult to work with. This chapter offers some specific guidelines for dealing with situations like these. As you work with writers, you will begin to develop your own repertoire of strategies for dealing with tricky or uncomfortable tutoring sessions.

THE WRITER WHO SEEKS HELP AT THE LAST MINUTE

You will sometimes encounter a writer who seeks help just before his paper is due. Perhaps the paper is due in two hours and the writer has only an incomplete draft with significant problems. Or, the paper is due tomorrow morning and the writer has no clue how to begin. Such writers may come to you in a guilty panic. How might you help?

DO

- ✓ Be kind and sympathetic. Help the writer sort through options and figure out what he can reasonably do in the time remaining.
- ✓ Help the writer consider other options. If it is not possible to complete an acceptable paper by the deadline, is receiving an extension an option? Is there a penalty for turning in a late paper?
- ✓ Help the writer set goals for future papers. When is the next paper due? Can the writer come in with an outline or a draft a week prior to the due date?

DON'T

✗ Scold or lecture the writer about the need to write papers in a timely manner; you may mean well, but the writer already knows what he has done wrong. At this point the writer needs to think clearly and, with your help, figure out the best way to cope with the situation.

THE UNRESPONSIVE WRITER

Teachers sometimes require students to visit the writing center, and occasionally, such a writer comes with an attitude of resistance. She may refuse to answer your questions, give halfhearted answers, or otherwise indicate that she does not wish to be there. Often, even her body language is telling. She may slump in her seat, avoid eye contact, or avoid facing you. How might you help?

DO

✓ Be patient and polite.
✓ Remind the writer that you are there to help and that the suggestions you offer are just that—suggestions that she may choose to accept or reject.
✓ Try to make the tutoring session short but helpful. If you can improve one aspect of a resistant writer's paper, perhaps she will see that coming to the writing center is not a waste of time.
✓ Engage the writer as much as possible. For example, have the writer read the paper aloud.
✓ Recognize that even your best efforts may not change a writer's attitude, at least in the initial tutoring session. With hindsight, a resistant writer may realize that getting help with a paper is not altogether unpleasant. Another day, she may return of her own volition.

DON'T

✗ Lecture the writer about your role or her unresponsiveness.

✗ Lose your cool and become angry.

✗ Become unresponsive as well. Try to keep the upper hand in this situation.

THE ANTAGONISTIC WRITER

For some writers, composing a paper looms as an extremely frustrating—perhaps even impossible—task. You may meet a writer who is apprehensive about writing in general or upset about demands placed on him by a particular assignment or teacher. Often, he views meeting these demands as being beyond his control. If someone could only tell him exactly how to "fix" things, all would be well. Finding himself in an impossible position, this writer may become verbally aggressive, redirecting his anger and frustration at you, or he may show little interest in the suggestions that you offer.

DO

✓ Be patient, polite, and supportive.

✓ Allow the writer to vent his feelings and tell you what is upsetting him.

✓ Acknowledge the writer's anger and difficulties with an *I* statement like "I hear how frustrated you are."

✓ Using an *I* statement, rephrase what the writer is saying in order to help him identify his emotions and problems. You might say, for example, "What I'm hearing is that you're discouraged because you can't figure out how to begin this paper."

✓ If noises or other distractions interfere with the session, move to a quieter place.

✓ If a writer becomes verbally aggressive, politely tell him that you are not willing to accept such behavior, but do so using an *I* statement. You might say, "When you yell at me that way, I find it difficult [impossible] to listen."

✓ Remind the writer that you are there to help and that the suggestions you offer are just that—suggestions that he may choose to accept or reject.

DON'T

✗ Lecture the writer about your role or his behavior.

✗ Get into an argument or a shouting match.

✗ Become hostile or punitive with statements like "You can't talk to me like that!"

✗ Look away and refuse to deal with the situation.

✗ Agree with any judgments and criticisms of assignments, teachers, and grades. Remember that doing so would be unprofessional.

THE WRITER WHO SELECTS AN INAPPROPRIATE TOPIC OR USES OFFENSIVE LANGUAGE

Occasionally, you may work with writers whose papers are laced inappropriately with offensive language, such as racist or sexist terms. Or you may have difficulty tutoring a writer with a paper that takes what you find to be an extreme and offensive position. How might you help?

DO

✓ Be patient and polite.
✓ Remind the writer that she is writing for an academic community, and ask her to consider how her audience will react to the language or topic.
✓ Respond as a reader and suggest, for example, "Some people might be disturbed by what you say here."
✓ Ask the writer to respond as a reader. Ask the writer to identify the audience. Then, say something like "Okay, imagine yourself as a member of your audience. How might you respond to this statement? Are you considering all potential responses to this paper?"
✓ Show the writer how to make language more acceptable. You can explain options for avoiding sexist language and suggest alternative terms or ways of rephrasing (many websites, handbooks, and guides to writing include sections on avoiding and eliminating sexist language, and you might want to refer the writer to such discussions).
✓ Occasionally, the writer may insist on her right to say what she wishes and decline to make any changes. You might suggest to her that she check with her teacher about the topic (or use of language) before continuing to work on the paper.

DON'T

✗ Become angry or hostile.
✗ Take the writer's viewpoints or language personally.
✗ Refuse to deal with the situation.

If you feel personally threatened or unsafe in any way, or if your strong feelings about a stance or position taken in a paper prohibit you from tutoring effectively, you should feel free to remove yourself from the tutoring session. You can gracefully explain that because of your personal values you may not be the most effective reader. If possible, work with the director to arrange for another tutor.

THE WRITER WHO PLAGIARIZES

Defining *plagiarism* is difficult at best. Discussions of it often conflate the deliberate use of someone else's work with problems of summarizing, paraphrasing, and documenting sources. On its website www.wpacouncil.org, the Council of Writing Program Administrators (WPA) offers the following definition: "In an instructional setting, plagiarism occurs when a writer deliberately uses someone else's language, ideas, or other original (not common-knowledge) material without acknowledging its source." It applies this definition to "texts published in print or on-line, to manuscripts, and to the work of other student writers." It also distinguishes between deliberate appropriation and the "misuse of sources," explaining that "[a] student who attempts (even if clumsily) to identify and credit his or her source, but who misuses a specific citation format or incorrectly uses quotation marks or other forms of identifying material from other sources, has not plagiarized. Instead, such a student should be considered to have failed to cite and document sources appropriately."

In the writing center, you will likely encounter writers who have committed plagiarism across the spectrum of "intentional" and "unintentional," an issue that may be complicated by people's use of the Web and perceptions of online authorship. Many students are very familiar with web writing, such as blogs or wikis, and consider such formats "community" writing. In the online world, borrowing language without citation is often considered acceptable. But the culture of authorship online is different from the culture of authorship in academic settings, and you may need to explain this distinction to some writers.

As a tutor, you should become familiar with your institution's code of academic integrity, with its definitions of academic dishonesty, and with the guidelines that it uses to enforce them. At some schools, tutors must report their suspicions of plagiarism; at other schools, tutors may explain what plagiarism is and advise writers to be careful about how they use and document information. How might you help?

DO

- ✓ Be familiar with your school's academic code of integrity.
- ✓ Be familiar with your writing center's resources (manuals, handbooks, handouts, online explanations) for properly summarizing, paraphrasing, and documenting information.
- ✓ Explain the importance of carefully taking notes from sources. Remind the writer to indicate the author's words clearly and to gather accurately all information that might be required for a citation.
- ✓ If you encounter a suspicious passage or phrase, explain that the text sounds "different" or "funny" and seems to be taken from another source. Explain that material taken from another source that is not

common knowledge must be documented, whether it is quoted directly, paraphrased, or summarized.

✓ Keep in mind that some writers concentrate on content in early drafts and do not include all information for citing portions of their papers at that stage; they add those details later. Or, an entire class may be responding to the same reading(s), and the teacher may have said that citations are therefore not necessary in this paper. If you are unsure, ask the writer for more information about the citation requirements for that assignment.

✓ Explain that acknowledging sources is an ethical issue, a matter of giving credit for ideas and/or words to the person who came up with them. Documenting sources appropriately both acknowledges the original writer and allows readers to locate that resource easily if so desired. Remember that this policy applies to web writing as well.

✓ Speak with your director or supervisor if you are unsure about how to handle a suspected case of plagiarism.

DON'T

✗ Accuse a writer directly of plagiarism.

THE WRITER WITH THE "PERFECT" PAPER

The "perfect" paper really is not a problem because it does not exist. Even if the paper seems to meet all the criteria for the assignment and the writer has expressed his thoughts well, you can still encourage the writer to look for areas that might be improved.

For a paper that is quite strong, some refining at the editing and revision stage can make the paper even more effective. Usually, such refinements amount to tweaking the paper at the sentence level. Furthermore, for some writers, effective writing is more intuitive than conscious. It also may be helpful for the writer to reflect on the strong aspects of the paper. Consciousness of these good writing skills and patterns can then be transferred to future papers.

On the other hand, you may encounter a writer who is confident that he has written the perfect paper and may even announce that fact. Rather than challenge that statement, a good place to start is to praise aspects that appear to be well done, then ease into pointing out places where there is room for improvement. Responding as a reader works well in such instances, for you can note an inviting introduction and good transitional sentences, then identify one or two places where the evidence, sentence structure, or word choice

could be even stronger. Once you work through one or two issues, he may be
more open to the revising process. How might you help?

DO

- ✓ Ask the writer which areas he thinks need more work. Being more
  familiar with the material and topic of the paper, the writer may know
  specifically what part needs stronger development.
- ✓ See what stylistic changes might be made, like combining sentences
  or shifting a phrase for better emphasis.
- ✓ Examine vocabulary carefully. Where might a better, more precise
  word replace an already good word?
- ✓ Identify and discuss particularly strong passages with the writer.

DON'T

- ✗ Assure the writer that he has an excellent paper, or guess at the grade
  the paper will receive. High praise may seem to be in order, but it
  should come from the teacher, not you. Remember that you may be
  unaware of some aspect of the assignment that may influence the
  grade.

THE WRITER WITH THE LONG PAPER

You will see a variety of paper topics, genres, and lengths in the writing center. This diversity is part of the fun of tutoring! But it can also be a challenge. The majority of writers you tutor in the writing center will likely bring in papers less than ten pages long. However, occasionally you will encounter a writer with a much longer paper, perhaps a capstone paper or honors thesis. Along with the writer, your task is to identify what the two of you can reasonably accomplish in a session, which usually means focusing on a particular aspect or portion of the paper. How might you help?

DO

- ✓ Find out if your writing center has a policy on paper length; some writing centers set limits on pages per session, while others ask that writers submit longer papers ahead of time so that tutors can read them beforehand.
- ✓ Ask the writer to prioritize the writing difficulties that she is having.
- ✓ Ask the writer to identify a manageable portion of the paper that may be fairly representative of these writing difficulties.
- ✓ Suggest that the writer return to the writing center with another section of the paper after she has further revised her writing.

DON'T

- ✗ Feel obligated to "get through" the entire paper. This will only force you to rush through the session and potentially overwhelm the writer.

We invite you to look at Appendix C and role-play some different tutoring scenarios. The exercise below also helps you to reconsider some of your own tutoring sessions that were not as successful as you might have liked.

EXERCISE 7A: Reflecting on Various Tutoring Situations

Think about a tutoring session in which you were not satisfied with the outcome. What made the situation so unpleasant, both for you and for the writer? How did you handle the situation? What are some other ways you might have handled it? Now think about a tutoring session in which you were satisfied with the outcome. What made the situation pleasant for both you and the writer? What did you learn from this encounter and how might it help you navigate future difficult tutoring sessions?

8

Research in the Writing Center

Many writing centers engage in some form of research; that is to say, tutors and staff investigate data and practices to challenge presumptions, extend our understanding, and sometimes reach new conclusions about the strategies and theories integral to our daily work in the writing center.

For some, research is very local, focused on the work and results of one writing center on one college or high school campus. For example, a writing center may collect data on student usage, analyze that data, and then revise policies or procedures to respond to the findings. Perhaps the data show that they are getting a disproportionate number of students from one course in a department. They decide to develop and offer a workshop series. Another writing center may present data to a dean or provost to demonstrate the need for increased staff or hours.

Often, writing centers participate in research that has the potential to influence the broader writing center community. For example, take the group of tutors who were interested in how plagiarism detection software—in this case, Turnitin—affected the writing culture on their campus. They investigated Turnitin's policies and practices and analyzed the results of a paper they ran through the software. Their essay—published in *The Writing Center Journal* and winner of the International Writing Centers Association 2007 "Best Article" award—raised awareness among the writing center community about the ethical considerations and pedagogical implications of using plagiarism detection software.[1]

In another example, a director was intrigued by a study published a decade earlier that investigated faculty's use of tutoring session reports. Using her writing center as a new case study, she first polled faculty to understand

---

[1] Brown, Renee, Brian Fallon, Elizabeth Matthews, and Elizabeth Mentie. "Taking on Turnitin: Tutors Advocating Change." *The Writing Center Journal* 27.1 (2007): 7–28.

their current use of her writing center's session reports. After analyzing the results of the survey, she provided faculty workshops on five specific strategies for using session reports. Finally, she surveyed faculty again to gauge if those new strategies were being used effectively.[2]

Because they are shared at conferences and disseminated via publications, results from research projects like these contribute to further developments in writing center practice and theory. Moreover, other writing centers can extend this research further, perhaps replicating a study from another university, exploring an unanswered question presented in a published essay, or challenging what is sometimes referred to as writing center "lore"—those practices that *seem* like good ideas, but haven't been closely studied in validated ways.

Conducting research is an exciting and valuable activity, but it can also be overwhelming and confusing! This chapter will provide you with a *basic* overview of the research process, beginning with formulating a research question and ending with potential publication venues. In Chapter 9, we provide more information about the various writing center communities that will support this research. Please don't think about the steps outlined below as stages of research you must complete fully and "conquer" before moving on to the next stage. Like the writing process, research is recursive: you will revisit your research question, add to your literature review, and tweak your methods as you go about conducting your research. Moreover, like so much of the work of the writing center, research is best when it is collaborative! Take advantage of the many perspectives and resources available to you in your writing center: throughout your research, talk to other tutors and confer with your director.

FORMULATING A RESEARCH QUESTION

One of the first steps in conducting research is figuring out what you wish to study and learn more about. When considering what topic to explore, start with what you know and are interested in! Think about subjects you've discussed or researched for your tutor training class, situations you've encountered while tutoring, writing center initiatives you've been involved in, and thoughts or conversations you've had after reading an article or book or hearing a speaker.

Formulating a research question is a bit like assessing the porridge in "Goldilocks and the Three Bears." Questions that are too broad—"Are writing centers effective?" or "Do students want to use the writing center?"—are in some ways unanswerable. With too many factors and aspects to consider,

---

[2]Cordaro, Danielle. "Practical Uses for Session Reports among Faculty: A Case Study." *The Writing Lab Newsletter* 38.9-10 (May/June 2014): 1–6.

you will quickly become overwhelmed. Questions that are too narrow—"Do Professor Hartman's students who use the writing center get more A's?" or "Why do students come to the writing center this semester more on Tuesdays than Fridays?"—are certainly answerable, but the answers don't yield interesting results beyond that idiosyncratic situation at your writing center.

To write a research question that is "just right," you will need to do some preliminary research to see in what ways this topic has already been explored. As you discuss your potential topic with your director or other tutors and read through different sources from journals and books, consider how your research might offer a "fresh" take on the topic. You want your research to address an area or question that you feel writing center research has not already fully explored or answered, or one that can benefit from being revisited. Moreover, you want to offer your audience a new or deeper way to think about their work in the writing center. In short, your goal as you conduct this preliminary research and draft your research question is to figure out how you can contribute to the scholarly conversation already taking place around this topic.

CONDUCTING A LITERATURE REVIEW

After you draft your research question, you'll want to dig deeper into the scholarship by conducting a literature review. In doing your preliminary research you get a "sense" of the scholarly conversation; in conducting a literature review, you become an expert. How? By reading broadly and deeply and by synthesizing what you find in your research. Conducting a literature review is critical for your understanding: it helps you find contextual and background information on your topic; it reveals the prevailing theoretical perspectives on your topic; it presents the variety of research methods applied to explore your topic; it shows the range of disciplines interested in your topic. And, most important, it shows the gaps that your research will fill.

You'll want to start the literature review early—it takes time to amass, read, and process the amount of material you will need to cover! Using key terms in your research question and from relevant theories and concepts, search for scholarship through your library databases. Ask a librarian for help in narrowing or broadening the results. If you use a general online search engine, remember the advice we gave in Chapter 6 on evaluating sources. And don't forget that your director and other tutors may have interesting sources to share as well.

As you read, take careful notes and document everything. Pause in your research every so often to write up and synthesize what you have read. Refine your research question if you need to. Return to the library if you need to. If you notice a scholar or study is repeatedly cited, find that essay.

Finally . . . stop! Any scholar will tell you that conducting the literature review can feel endless, and you will need to discern when you are ready to move on to your own research study. Remember that you can always go back and add to your literature review as needed.

SELECTING YOUR METHODS AND CONDUCTING YOUR RESEARCH

Research is like an adventure: you need to be prepared with a detailed plan before you embark. What path will you take? What tools and provisions will you need? Will you be traveling solo or with a team? Developing a research plan, complete with a timeline, will help you set off on your course of research with confidence.

The first thing you need to consider is your methodology. Your methods need to be appropriate for the data you are trying to collect. Moreover, some disciplines value one method over another; pay close attention to methods as you conduct your literature review to determine this!

Quantitative research relies on the statistical, numerical, or mathematical analysis of collected data in order to arrive at generalizations across groups of people or explanations for particular phenomena. Those who do quantitative research claim a certain level of objectivity; that is to say, "the numbers speak for themselves." Quantitative methods may include polls, questionnaires, surveys, and statistical data.

Qualitative research is used to understand people's behaviors and actions within their natural setting, and qualitative researchers are particularly interested in social interactions and phenomena. Like quantitative research, qualitative research also involves the collection of evidence; however, it seeks more to explore the questions "why" or "how" instead of "what," "where," or "when." Qualitative methods may include interviews, observation, focus groups, field notes, and document analysis.

Mixed methods research combines quantitative and qualitative methods. The researcher selects methods from each intentionally, so that the combination of quantitative and qualitative data helps her gather evidence that can both *measure* "known" phenomena and causal relationships and *explore* explanations and understandings of why and how such phenomena occur.

After you decide on your methods, you will need to figure out your sample size: are you conducting a case study of one writer? Or are you polling the entire first-year class? What are the time constraints or other restrictions that your sample study dictates? Moreover, will you need a budget? If you are conducting a focus group, for example, you probably want to include light snacks. And sometimes people are compensated—with money or a gift card—for participating in interviews or filling out a long survey.

Most research requires you to go through your institution's Institutional Review Board (IRB) process. The specific IRB process may be different from school to school, but, overall, the role of an IRB is to evaluate research projects to ensure that they will be conducted ethically and within the regulations set by the school. Receiving IRB approval can take time, so start paperwork early in your process.

Understand that research is a fluid thing and may take many semesters and many tutors over time to complete. You might complete just one small stage, and that's okay. The checklist below can be helpful as you formulate your research plan and seek out support and collaboration from your director and/or other tutors.

WHAT IS YOUR GOAL? WHY DO YOU WANT TO CONDUCT RESEARCH?

✓ To earn academic credit?
✓ To influence pedagogy on your campus?
✓ To influence the broader field/discipline beyond your campus?
✓ To gain experience with certain research methods?
✓ As preparation for graduate school or a profession?
✓ For publication?

WHO COMPRISES YOUR RESEARCH TEAM?

Even if the majority of the work of the research is done by you, you should still think about who can and will support your work.

✓ Who will be your mentor? A faculty member? A graduate student? An administrator?
✓ Will you have coresearchers? Other students? Faculty? Community members?
✓ What additional academic resources will you use? Librarians? Institutional Review Board (IRB)? Previous researchers? Researchers/students/faculty at another institution?
✓ Don't forget emotional resources! What family and friends can give you a boost when you need it?

HAVE YOU APPROPRIATELY VETTED YOUR RESEARCH QUESTION AND RESEARCH DESIGN WITH YOUR RESEARCH TEAM?

✓ Have you made any appropriate changes?

DO YOU HAVE A GOOD HANDLE ON THE CURRENT SCHOLARSHIP INFORMING YOUR RESEARCH?

✓ Have you conducted a proper literature review?
✓ Have you vetted that literature review with your mentor?
✓ Have you fully explored scholarship in other disciplines that may influence your research?

WHAT IS YOUR TIMELINE?

✓ A semester?
✓ One year?
✓ Greater than one year?

WHAT ARE THE FUNDING CONSIDERATIONS?

✓ Does your research require funding? (for computational models, tools)
✓ Might your research require funding? (for compensation for participation, for food, for travel)
✓ Can you apply for grants to support your research?

DO YOU NEED IRB APPROVAL?

✓ Are you sure?
✓ Have you allowed for sufficient time in your research design for IRB approval? (This can take months.)

HAVE YOU SET UP AN ADEQUATE ACCOUNTABILITY MECHANISM?

✓ Meeting with your mentor regularly
✓ Writing up segments of your research as you complete it

HAVE YOU "STAGED" THE DISSEMINATION OF YOUR RESEARCH?

✓ On-campus forums
✓ Community forums
✓ Regional conferences
✓ National/International conferences
✓ On-campus publications
✓ Community publications
✓ Scholarly publications

SHARING YOUR RESEARCH

Sharing your research is vitally important, helping you to gather feedback at different stages of your research and giving you an opportunity to influence the discipline. You have a variety of ways you can share your research: at a staff meeting; at a campus forum; at regional, national, or international conferences; or within one of the many writing center publications. What forum you select depends on the kind of feedback you need, where you are in the research process, and what you hope to accomplish in disseminating your research. Since your research is such a critical part of your professional development as a tutor, and because we understand how intimidating that can be, we share the following detailed suggestions for this important professional activity.

Conference Presentations

Conferences allow professionals in a field to come together and discuss common issues, share ideas, learn new approaches, and establish and maintain connections with one another. All writing center conferences encourage peer tutors to participate, both as attendees and as presenters. If you are attending a conference, then you simply need to pay attention to the registration date and make travel plans. If you hope to present at a conference in order to share your research and gain feedback from a wide network of professionals, then what follows should be helpful as you prepare.

PREPARING THE PROPOSAL. Months ahead of time, conference organizers publish a Call for Proposals (CFP) that explains the options for presentations and the requirements for submitting a proposal, like the length and due date. Most conferences feature a theme. While not all presentations must adhere to that theme, you can often find a link between the theme and an area of interest to you, or the theme can serve as a springboard to help you find and consider possible topics for a presentation. (One tip: Be careful not to overdo references to the theme in your proposal; persons reviewing proposals quickly tire of forced or overdone references.)

You will be asked to choose a presentation type; the chart on page 118 explains typical options, and you should select the one that best fits the content you plan to address. The presentation type you select will also influence the amount of time you have and your methods of delivery. What can you reasonably do in the time allotted? In thirty minutes, for example, you could not possibly deal with the topic "difficult tutoring situations," but you could select one or two kinds of difficult sessions to discuss. Do you want to explain an approach to the audience, for example, or do you want them to engage in an exercise or activity and then discuss the implications of what they observed or learned?

Your task in a proposal is to demonstrate to reviewers that (1) the subject is worthwhile, (2) you have foundational knowledge about the subject, (3) you have something new or interesting to contribute about the subject, and (4) you have thought through how you will communicate your ideas to the audience and involve them. Proposals are reviewed by a group of people in the field who usually decide whether to accept, reject, or accept with suggested changes. These suggestions are included when you are informed about your proposal's status.

Most conferences have an online form for proposals that typically requires the following information:

- **An informative title** that tells attendees the gist of your presentation. Avoid vague titles, like "The Flavor of Tutoring," for they tell attendees nothing about your presentation. Likewise, remember that a title should be able to fit on one or two lines of a program.

Types of Conference Presentations

Type	Definition	Time
Individual Presentations	3–4 individual papers grouped (often by conference organizers) around a topic or theme. Each member speaks for a designated, predetermined amount of time and questions may follow.	15–20 minutes for each speaker in a 45- to 75-minute time slot
Panel Presentations	3+ speakers (usually preselected) on a topic, theme, or different aspects of a topic or theme. Each member speaks for a predetermined, designated amount of time, followed by general discussion and/or questions.	15–20 minutes for each speaker in a 45- to 75-minute time slot
Roundtable Discussion	4+ "equal" speakers (hence the name roundtable), each speaking in turn on a topic/theme or aspects of a topic/theme. Speakers typically read from notes and respond to each other extemporaneously. May be followed by questions and/or discussion.	45 to 75 minutes
Poster	Visual presentation of information and/or ideas, often with time allotted for the presenter to talk with individuals about the work.	May be displayed throughout the conference or for a specified time.
Workshop	A short statement on a topic, followed by involving the audience in an activity, often in pairs or groups. Workshop leaders provide attendees with questions or scenarios (written, online, videotaped, or acted out) to discuss and actively involve them in sharing ideas about and experiences with a topic.	Can vary in length from 45 minutes to a half or full day.

- **Contact information for all presenters**: names, addresses, phone numbers, e-mail addresses, and institutional affiliations.
- **An abstract** that explains the focus of your presentation in a few sentences. Often these abstracts appear in the program. Along with the title, attendees use them to decide which presentations interest them, so follow guidelines for length and make them succinct.
- **A description** of your presentation that adheres to the prescribed length. Your discussion might include references that indicate your knowledge of

MUTTS © 2004 Patrick McDonnell King Features Syndicate, Inc.

the theoretical underpinnings for your argument, a brief explanation of methods applied to answer the questions you've posed, and references to the evidence used to support your claims. If you plan to involve the audience, explain how. If your presentation includes several presenters, you will likely need to explain each individual's contribution. As you write, be aware that reviewers of proposals come from other writing centers, so terms that have meaning in your writing center may be a mystery to someone from another. For example, a first-year writing course may be English 101 at one school and Writing 111 at another. Use more generic descriptions, like "first-year writing" or "composition courses" instead.

- **Any audiovisual equipment** that you will require.

PREPARING THE PRESENTATION. Once your proposal has been accepted, you will need to decide exactly how your presentation will proceed. Create a brief outline and break it down by time, especially if you have multiple speakers or plan to involve the audience in activities and feedback. For example, if your presentation involves audience participation, you might plan as follows:

5 min.	Introduction (Speaker A)
10 min.	Activity 1
10 min.	Discussion of Activity 1 (Led by Speaker A)
5 min.	Introduce Activity 2 (Speaker B)
10 min.	Activity 2
10 min.	Discussion of Activity 2 (Led by Speaker B)
5 min.	Questions (Speaker A & Speaker B)

As you draft your presentation, remember that institutions differ. Don't assume that all writing centers are alike. The size of a school and its tutoring staff affects many aspects of how the writing center operates, and may require brief explanations to establish context. For example, mandatory weekly tutor meetings work well for maintaining communication in centers with ten to fifteen tutors, but those with staffs of fifty to sixty must find other ways to keep in regular contact. Similarly, you might need to explain that your writing center is open only evenings in dorms or operates only on a walk-in basis or serves mostly older, nontraditional students. If your center goes by a name that might be unfamiliar to your audience, like "The Annex" or "The Write Place," explain your references at the start. Remember, too, that course numbers and names differ from school to school, so use terminology that everyone will recognize such as "the first-year writing course."

So that you are familiar and comfortable with it, practice your presentation, preferably before an audience of supportive, yet honest, friends and colleagues. Be sure to time your talk and make changes so that you can fit everything into the allotted time frame. Get feedback and make adjustments.

Consider visual aids, perhaps a PowerPoint or handout that might enhance your presentation. If you opt for a PowerPoint, be sure to keep it simple and use a font large enough that the audience can read it. Be aware that you must pay extra to use technical equipment at some conferences, so budget that in or consider alternatives. In addition, anticipate the occasional technological failure with a backup plan. If your salient points or relevant quotations will be presented using a projector or PowerPoint, prepare handouts that you can use if the equipment fails. Bring at least enough copies so that people can share, and be sure to have hard copies of everything for yourself. On any handout that you provide for participants, make sure that you include the title of your talk, your name, and your e-mail address so that participants can contact you later. Finally, bring a couple of extra copies for any attendees who may be hearing impaired, so that they can easily read along as you present.

ARRIVING AT THE CONFERENCE. When you arrive at the conference, check in at the registration table, where you will receive a program, name tag, and other pertinent information. If you haven't already done so with an online program, sit down with the hard copy, figure out which sessions are "must attend," and decide which others look promising. See what other professional or social activities might be planned; Special Interest Groups or SIGs, for example, offer opportunities to meet like-minded people from other writing centers, while an opening reception or early morning running group may allow you to network and make new friends. Throughout the conference, consider carrying a bottle of water and a few granola bars or other snacks; at some conferences food is expensive and/or not readily available.

DELIVERING THE PRESENTATION. If you can, check out the physical setup of the room where you will be presenting beforehand. Will you be speaking from a podium? From behind a table? Are seats for the audience fixed or movable? Troubleshoot and make last-minute adjustments, if necessary. For example, fixed seats may not work well for a planned group activity, so you may want to have people work in pairs instead. If you plan to use electronic equipment like an overhead projector or a computer, check the equipment. Is it in working order and compatible with your material? Where is it positioned? Would it be helpful to have someone else flip through PowerPoint slides for you or pass out handouts?

All presenters, even experienced ones, are nervous, which often means that they tend to talk quickly. Before you begin, take a deep breath, smile, and remind yourself to speak slowly. Some conferences encourage reading a paper; for others, it is more appropriate to speak more informally from notes. In any case, be sure you look up and make eye contact as you speak. If you will be speaking from notes, practice enough beforehand to ensure you adhere strictly to the time limits set. If you are part of a panel of presenters and you go over by even a few minutes, someone else must cut their presentation as they speak.

Often, several people presenting on similar topics are grouped together for a session; thus, when you present or during the question-answer time, you may be able to refer to parts of the other presentations. As others speak, keep a pen and paper handy to jot down notes that you might later use as you refer to those connections.

People in the audience often wander in and out during presentations, especially if two or three presentations are grouped together as a panel. This behavior is acceptable, and you should not consider it an affront to you or your presentation.

CHAIRING A SESSION. Most conferences ask for volunteers to "chair" a session, which typically involves introducing speakers, keeping track of time, and moderating questions. Ask the presenters how they wish to be introduced, and confirm that they will be speaking in the order that is listed on the program. If there are any changes, be sure to announce them at the opening of the session. Often, a panel prefers to do its own introductions, so you may need only to introduce the session. Session panels feature several speakers, each allotted a set amount of time, and you will need to warn each when they have five minutes left to speak, then again when they have one minute. Position yourself so that you can unobtrusively show the speaker warnings that say "5 min." and "1 min." (You can write the numbers on a piece of paper and hold them up or you can simply raise your hand or a finger.) Other session formats—workshops or roundtables, for example—will only need you to keep track of the overall time to ensure there is ten to fifteen minutes left for questions.

When you moderate questions, be aware of the session's ending time so that people can move to another session and the next presenters can get ready. A gracious way to end is to say, "We have time for one more question." Remember to thank the presenters as you end the session.

PUBLISHING YOUR RESEARCH

Several respected journals offer opportunities for tutors to publish a range of essays, from presentations of research projects and studies to reflections on aspects of tutoring writing. Each journal offers guidelines for length, documentation, and stylistic preferences. In addition to reviewing and abiding by these guidelines, take the time to read through recent editions of the publication to get a feel for the overall tone and style of the essays.

Just as each cover letter should be revised for each prospective job or graduate school, your essay should be written with the journal and its audience in mind. In most cases, a promising manuscript is juried; that is, two or more external readers review it to decide if it is publishable. If they think it is, they may offer questions or suggestions to the author to help with revising.

When you submit a manuscript, it should be your *very best work*. As scholars draft articles in their fields, they often share them with colleagues to get feedback beforehand. You might turn to your mentors or other tutors for their suggestions. Expect to do many, many drafts to produce a well-researched, carefully thought out, polished version, and don't be surprised if reviewers still have suggestions for clarification or more development.

The journals below publish research specific to writing center work; however, the list is by no means exhaustive. Depending on your research, there may be other writing center journals or publications in other disciplines that would welcome your contribution.

- *Writing Center Journal (WCJ):* Published twice yearly, *WCJ* includes articles on issues and trends of interest to tutors and writing center administrators. It also features a blog.
- *WLN: A Journal of Writing Center Scholarship:* Published ten times a year, *WLN* features articles also of interest to tutors and writing center administrators and includes a tutor column.
- *Young Scholars in Writing:* Published annually, this refereed journal is dedicated to publishing research articles written by undergraduates in disciplines associated with rhetoric, writing, and/or literacy studies.
- *The Dangling Modifier:* Published twice a year, this international newsletter by and for peer tutors in writing provides a forum for ongoing conversation about peer tutoring. *The Dangling Modifier* is produced in association with the National Conference on Peer Tutoring in Writing (NCPTW).
- *Praxis:* A peer-reviewed scholarly journal published biannually by the University Writing Center at the University of Texas at Austin, *Praxis* welcomes articles from writing center consultants, administrators, and

others concerned with issues related to writing center training, consulting, labor, administration, and initiatives.

WHY RESEARCH?

Research offers you an opportunity to think through and research your ideas, then make a contribution to the field by communicating your findings to others. Presenting at conferences and publishing extends your research beyond the borders of your campus as you then contribute in a meaningful way to your writing center and to our discipline.

It is important for you to know that how research is defined, and what "counts" as research depends greatly on disciplinary considerations and the cultural or institutional context of your writing center. However narrowly or broadly you define your research, we are sure you will find the process challenging and rewarding.

EXERCISE 8A: Researching Tutoring Strategies

In this book, we've introduced many strategies for tutoring. Go through each chapter and look for some tutoring strategies that could be substantiated — or challenged! — with research. Choose one, do some preliminary research, and find at least three sources that address the tutoring strategy. Do the authors offer additional suggestions or ideas?

EXERCISE 8B: "Where We Stand On . . ." Critical Literature Review Research Paper on Current Writing Center Topic

This assignment has two parts and is designed to help you explore the research on a topic and figure out what additional research may be conducted. In total, it should be about eight to ten pages. Select a writing center topic that interests you. First, write a critical literature review, considering the following questions:

1. What is the research "history" and evolution of this topic? When did interest in this topic begin? How was research **framed** at that time? Did **key terms** shift/change? Where was this research **published**? Which **disciplines** informed this research? What seemed to be the predominate **theories** of influence?

2. What does the current scholarship (within the past five to ten years) say about this topic? Are the answers to #1 different today? (Framing?

Key terms? Publication venues? Influential disciplines? Theories of influence?)

Second, conclude by suggesting what research needs to be started and/or continued in writing centers to further the disciplinary conversation on your topic. Include potential research questions and research methods.

EXERCISE 8C: Analyzing a Research Study

Find a published study in one of the writing center journals. Analyze the research conducted: Why did the author state that he initiated the research study? What was included in the literature review? What were the author's methods? How did the author analyze the results? Did the author pose any questions for further study?

9

The Writing Center as a Community

As a writing tutor, you now belong to a very special professional community: Welcome! In fact, tutoring writing is one of the few truly professional activities in which a student—whether high school or college—can participate. One of the best things about tutoring is that it is never stagnant. Because different writers come to a writing center with different assignments and different perspectives, no two sessions are ever the same. Even tutors who have been advising writers for many years recognize it as a professional activity in which they continue to learn and grow. We hope that you will not only take advantage of all that tutoring has to offer you, but also have fun, learn much, and enjoy being part of this community.

The first chapter of this guide, "The Writing Center as a Workplace," underscores some important professional considerations you should attend to as you work with writers, specifically issues relating to ethical behavior and employability skills. This final chapter, "The Writing Center as a Community," invites you to join other writing tutors in sharing ideas and experiences, and in making important contributions to our professional scholarly and disciplinary community.

Happily, we are a collaborative and friendly profession, one that welcomes members at all levels—secondary school; college or university undergraduate or graduate; professional; administrative—and one that embraces members throughout the world. Around the globe, people connect on local, regional, national, and international levels, as social media, meetings, conferences, and publications foster communication, and allow members to exchange ideas, ask questions, and learn from one another. We urge you to explore becoming an active member of this community.

To begin, consider the various networks that exist for your writing center, from local to global. Can you collaborate and share resources with other writing centers in your city or town? Even just a friendly visit to a local writing center can yield productive relationships and open your eyes to alternative approaches and methods. Many writing centers in the United States belong to what is called a "regional" writing centers association, with regions comprised of a limited geographical area, usually neighboring states. The authors of this book belong to the Mid-Atlantic Writing Centers Association, or MAWCA. Most regionals maintain a website and social media, host a yearly conference, publish newsletters, sponsor professional meetings and activities, and provide mentorship and support. Moreover, regionals can provide wonderful leadership opportunities for peer tutors, with representation on their boards and committees. In addition to the ten or so regionals found in the United States, the European Writing Centers Association (EWCA) and the Middle East-North Africa Writing Centers Alliance (MENAWCA) support writing centers within the contexts of their respective communities. Others, too, like the Writing Centers Association of Japan and the South African Writing Centres, offer opportunities to share resources at meetings or online, even for people outside their geographic area.

Often, these regionals are affiliated with the International Writing Centers Association (IWCA), a National Council of the Teachers of English Assembly. The IWCA website — http://writingcenters.org — is a wonderful resource with timely and practical information about writing center work for peer, graduate, and professional tutors as well as for writing center directors. Here you can find position statements, job opportunities, news and updates, and a wide variety of resources, from tips for new directors to annotated bibliographies. It also provides links to the regional organizations, online journals, further resources for tutors and writers, and discussion forums. Consider joining IWCA; a membership includes reduced rate subscriptions to two important journals: *WLN: A Journal of Writing Center Scholarship* and *Writing Center Journal*. Reading publications will help you to stay abreast of issues and activities in the field.

The IWCA Website also gives details about discussion groups that focus on issues of particular interest to peer tutors, graduate students, administrators, and high school writing centers. Chief among these discussion forums is *Wcenter* — an open, friendly, international discussion group devoted to tutoring writing and other related issues. Blogs also connect peer writing tutors or consultants and those interested in collaborative learning: *PeerCentered*, for example, offers space to talk and share, as well as scheduled discussions on specific topics or with authors of relevant books and articles. *Connecting Writing Centers Across Borders*, sponsored by *WLN: A Journal of Writing Center Scholarship*, encourages interactions among writing center people across the globe, "especially those without nearby writing centers."

As the preceding chapter discusses, conferences serve as major forums for exchanging ideas, reporting on research, and focusing on specific collaborative learning topics, as well as connecting with old friends and making new ones. IWCA hosts conferences regularly, as do many regional groups or area consortiums, which are sometimes formed in countries, states, or cities. One notable example is the National Conference on Peer Tutoring in Writing (NCPTW), which has met annually in the United States since 1984. Whether small, perhaps just an afternoon gathering of people involved in tutoring at your school, or large, a longer, more formal meeting of writing tutors from a wide geographic area, conferences typically energize participants and allow them to share and learn more about how tutoring writing works in other places.

A common metaphor for a writing center is that of a "Burkean Parlor." It derives from a passage in *The Philosophy of Literary Form* (110–11) by Kenneth Burke that describes ongoing conversation about writing:

> Imagine that you enter a parlor. You come late. When you arrive, others have long preceded you, and they are engaged in a heated discussion, a discussion too heated for them to pause and tell you exactly what it is about. In fact, the discussion had already begun long before any of them got there, so that no one present is qualified to retrace for you all the steps that had gone before. You listen for a while, until you decide that you have caught the tenor of the argument; then you put in your oar. Someone answers; you answer him; another comes to your defense; another aligns himself against you, to either the embarrassment or gratification of your opponent, depending upon the quality of your ally's assistance. However, the discussion is interminable. The hour grows late, you must depart. And you do depart, with the discussion still vigorously in progress.[1]

As Andrea Lunsford noted in her seminal 1991 *Writing Center Journal* essay, "Collaboration, Control, and the Idea of a Writing Center,"[2] this metaphor also aptly describes the field of writing center practice and theory and captures the ideals of what we hope to achieve in each tutoring session. We hope you will take advantage of the many opportunities to join in and contribute to this ongoing conversation.

If you have worked your way through this book while actually tutoring, then you have been gathering your own repertoire of information about writing and helping writers. Whether you interact face-to-face or online, you likely know more about the writing process and have developed a sense of what is comfortable for you as a tutor. You can work — fairly easily, we hope —

---

[1]Burke, Kenneth. *The Philosophy of Literary Form*. Berkeley: University of California Press, 1941.
[2]Lunsford, Andrea. "Collaboration, Control, and the Idea of a Writing Center." *Writing Center Journal 12.1* (1991): 3–10.

with writers who have different learning styles, competencies, attitudes, and assignments; you can assess their needs and plan and manage a session, adapting even as dynamics change within a session.

You know what questions to ask and can make suggestions and give writers the tools to tackle their writing projects more confidently and successfully. Whether you tutor for a short time or for years, this repertoire of information will be developed and refined, but already you have begun cultivating your own philosophy of how to tutor effectively. Articulating that philosophy will help you to clarify it and reveal those places where you might want to read, talk, and think more about what it is that you do as a tutor.

EXERCISE 9A: Articulating Your Tutoring Philosophy

In a five- to six-page paper, reflect on your tutoring experiences thus far. Your paper should synthesize three areas: your work with writers; book and article readings about composition, tutoring, and writing centers; and your discussions—formal and informal—with other tutors. In determining a thesis and planning your paper, think about the intersections of these areas.

You may choose to write about tutoring in general, or you may focus on a particular issue to which you find yourself returning frequently, like tutoring multilingual writers or determining the agenda for sessions or underscoring writers' responsibility for their own papers. Or, you might discuss two or three sessions that were especially meaningful to you in light of readings and discussions. What is important is that you synthesize your tutoring experiences with writing center research in order to arrive at your own tutoring philosophy.

EXERCISE 9B: Creating a Metaphor for Tutoring

From William Shakespeare describing the world as "a stage" in *As You Like It* to Robert Burns declaring that "O my Love's like a red, red rose" ("A Red, Red Rose," 1794) to actress Katharine Hepburn saying she is like an oak tree to a tutor comparing herself with a flight attendant or a pastry chef, people use metaphors to compare unlike entities. Such comparisons range from simply noting a similarity to serving as a central idea and controlling image. The latter—an extended metaphor—often captures the beliefs or assumptions that underlie someone's attitudes or beliefs about the subject.

What follows is John's comparison of tutoring with jazz, one tutor's example of an extended metaphor.

> *Tutoring is like playing jazz. Improvisation and good timing are musts for jazz musicians, and the same holds true for tutors. During jazz improvisation periods, band members must be able to alter their style to fit the needs of the song. For example, a bass player must constantly be aware of the drummer's*

tempo because it could change at any time. If the bass player does not alter his playing to fit the drummer's rhythm, then the entire song sounds out of synch. Similarly, as the writer and tutor talk and work with a draft, the writer's needs could change at any time; if the tutor does not adapt to fit those needs then the session may not be as helpful as it could be.

Part of the bass player's responding to the drummer's change in tempo involves adaptability, and it's the same with the tutor's responding to the writer's needs. In both cases, you have to know enough to be able to shift gears, to change your way of approaching the song or of explaining things to the writer, and to do so on the spot.

Although jazz relies heavily on improvisation, all musicians also must be aware of the rules, or theory, of music, which correlates directly with how a tutor must approach a session; the tutor must always be cognizant of the major theories and philosophies of tutoring when working with a writer. These are the matters that play around in the background, but they are a significant and necessary part. Finding an appropriate mix of improvisation and theory is difficult in both jazz and tutoring; however, it is this very challenge that can make both experiences rewarding, pleasing, enjoyable, and successful.

Think of a metaphor that aptly describes tutoring for you or one that characterizes writing and the roles that tutors and writers play in the process. In a few paragraphs, extend that metaphor. Begin by stating that "tutoring is [like] X" and then explain how or why the two are similar. Share and discuss your metaphors with other tutors, and consider ways in which each might be extended even more.

This exercise is also an interesting one to do as a visual representation, using an image or creating a collage of pictures to depict your extended metaphor. These visual representations can even be displayed in your writing center!

APPENDIX A

Tutors Ask...

The following questions were posed by tutors. See what kinds of suggestions you can come up with for dealing with the situations they describe. If possible, share your ideas with other tutors. (You may use the questions as departure points for group discussion in class or online.)

1. What can I do to make writers do more of the work in a tutoring session? How can I help them discover more of the answers themselves? How do I do this in an online environment?

2. What can I do with papers that seem just fine? I worked with someone the other day, and I just couldn't come up with any real suggestions for improving the paper.

3. I had a writer who was working hard, but she kept talking about how she thought the assignment was just too difficult. I tried to sympathize, but I was afraid she'd think that I agreed with her. What could I have done?

4. What can I do if I don't fully understand the assignment? Online, I had the description of an assignment, but it was only two sentences! The writer tried to explain his assignment to me so I could help him get started, but he was so vague, and I couldn't really tell what the teacher was looking for.

5. What should I do when a lazy writer comes into the writing center assuming that the tutor will come up with all the ideas? I tried so hard to get this particular writer to think and come up with her own ideas, but she just sat there silently or said, "I don't know."

6. What can I do for people who come in ten or fifteen minutes before closing and can't come back the next day? Should I try to help them anyway? How?

7. Should I allow writers to walk out of the writing center with glaring errors still in their papers? What impression will teachers—or even those writers—have of the writing center when that happens?

8. In a session yesterday, I worked with a writer who was quite frustrated with his schoolwork, his assignments, and his professor. He was quite negative from the start. I could feel the tension. His body language and facial expressions indicated that he was feeling a great deal of stress. I got him to calm down a bit, and I basically let him air some of the gripes that he had. After letting off some steam, he seemed to feel a bit more relaxed and comfortable. What else can I do to help in this kind of situation? I felt like I spent most of the session just getting him to calm down. Wasn't this a waste of time? Was it worthwhile to have a tutoring session?

9. Some writers just want a quick fix and get impatient when I start explaining why something is wrong. How can I get someone to really listen when I explain these things?

10. A writer submitted a paper to the online writing center and only wrote that she wanted it "proofread." How do I know where to get started?

11. Sometimes a writer leaves with an attitude that suggests that I was of no help whatsoever. When this happens, how much should I blame myself? The writer? What can I do to avoid this kind of problem?

12. As I worked with a writer on a paper, I realized that not all the work was his. He wrote about some things he couldn't explain and used words he couldn't define. What's the best way to deal with a situation like this?

13. I'm taking a literary criticism course from a professor who also teaches a poetry class, and I tutored one of his students from that class the other day. Yesterday the professor stopped me and asked about that session. I had another class, so I couldn't stay to talk, but I felt very uncomfortable being asked about a tutoring session like that. What should I do if that happens again?

14. From a female tutor: A guy came in for help with a paper, but when I began to work with him, all he did was stare at me. He went so far as to compliment my appearance. I couldn't get him to focus on his paper. Pretty soon, I felt so uncomfortable I couldn't focus on his paper either. What could I have done?

15. What should I do if I'm scheduled to tutor someone from a class I'm taking, probably working on the same assignment I'm working on?

16. A student brought a paper that had already been graded. Though she said she wanted me to explain the teacher's comments, it quickly became apparent that she disagreed with the grade and really just wanted me

to support her point of view. I think she wanted to be able to go back to the professor and say, "The Writing Center says you're wrong." I did think the professor was rather harsh, but I didn't want to say that to the student. What's a good way to handle a situation like this?

17. A student brought in a take-home exam and wanted help. I wasn't sure if that was something I should do or not. Are there times when it might be okay? Times when it might not be?

18. Several weeks ago, a friend came to my dorm room. He wanted help with a paper because he knows I tutor at the writing center. I was studying for a test, but he was so desperate that I helped him for about an hour. When I saw him yesterday, he was mad because he got only a C on his paper. I gave up my study time and he's mad? How should I have handled this situation?

19. Every so often I get a writer who wants more help than I think I can give. I don't know much about what should be in essays of application for graduate school, for example. I don't want to look stupid, but I don't want to give someone advice that might not be very helpful. What should I do in a case like this?

20. I sometimes tutor students privately. One of them wanted to see me when I finished work at the writing center yesterday. She didn't have much time and wanted to work with me there. It didn't seem right, but I didn't know what to say to her.

21. We have a set time limit for our appointments, but sometimes a writer gets really pushy about wanting more time. How can I deal with a rude person without being rude myself?

22. I think I may have inadvertently offended someone when I was tutoring him in an online chat. I made a little joke, followed by LOL, and then there was just "silence" on the other end. In a face-to-face, I'd know how to recover, but in this situation, I had no idea what I did wrong or how to make it okay.

23. I work with the same writer every few days. Today I learned that he sees other tutors with the same paper between our appointments. I suspect he does little or nothing on his own; instead, he just takes the specific suggestions one tutor makes, then moves on to another tutor. What should I do?

24. Some writers expect me to be an expert on documentation. They ask me really specific questions, like "Should I have a comma or period here?" or "How do I cite a conference paper posted on someone's home page?" They seem to think I'm stupid for not having this information on the tip of my tongue. What do I say to them?

25. A writer came with her senior thesis and asked for a "final look-through." She was so proud of her paper and seemed to just want praise

for it. Unfortunately, her documentation was not only incomplete but also incorrect. I pointed that out in several places, but she insisted she had done everything her teacher had told her to do. What's a good way to handle this kind of "last minute," troublesome situation?

26. A writer asked for help with sentence structure in his paper. I did everything right—made sure he did all the writing as I suggested ways to rephrase sentences—but he made me feel as if I were dictating changes to him. He'd say, "That's good; tell me again slowly," and he'd write down my suggestions word-for-word then move on to the next sentence. What's a good way to handle a situation like this?

27. I helped a writer who was really nice and even fun to work with. As we finished the session, she asked for my e-mail address "in case she had more questions." I didn't know if I should give it to her or not.

28. I just started tutoring online and I'm surprised by how much time it takes! I spend two hours at least on each paper. I want to make sure I don't copyedit, but I feel compelled to address every issue.

29. A writer came for help on a research paper. She seemed fine at first—really willing to listen to suggestions—but several minutes into the session, she began to cry and said she just wasn't "good at research." I shared some of my own frustrations about writing but wondered what else I could have said to help her.

30. As I helped a multilingual writer with his paper, I realized he was thinking in his home language and then attempting to translate his words into English. While his ideas were fine, they got lost as he tried to put English words and phrases on paper. What are some good strategies for a situation like this? Also, am I allowed to provide him with words that he's having trouble finding, especially idioms?

31. I really enjoy tutoring and some of the writers I've worked with seem also to get a lot out of the tutoring session—so much so that a few have begun requesting me rather adamantly. I'm kind of embarrassed, but I also feel like I have a good handle on these writers' particular problems, since I see them often. Then again, some students seem to be getting dependent on me, scheduling multiple appointments ahead of time and making comments like, "We got a B+ on this one" and "I couldn't have done it without you." Is it okay for me to have "regulars"? How should I handle their future requests?

32. So I helped this writer the other day and we got through part of his paper. But he wanted more help and I wasn't scheduled for the next hour, so we kept working. But we still didn't finish, so I met him in the library and we worked again. It felt like too much time, but the paper just wasn't *done* even after all this time, and it needed more work. So, was this okay?

APPENDIX B

Tutors Talk: Evaluating What They Say

In each of the following examples, indicate what the tutor said or did that was or was not effective, and explain why. Describe what the tutor might have said or done instead. (You may use the examples as departure points for in-class or online group discussion.)

1. Wow! You have a problem with run-on sentences. Let me get you a worksheet that explains how to fix them and an exercise to practice with. When you finish, let me know and I'll correct it.

2. Hi, I'm Eric. Let's sit down over here. You can put your book bag there and then tell me what you're working on.

3. Help you . . . now? We usually take people on the hour. I've just tutored two people and I'm tired. Besides, I have an econ exam this afternoon, and I was hoping to get a few minutes to review stuff. How much help do you need?

4. Here, in your paper, you say that "most upper-level courses require research papers." If you really want to convince your audience, you need to support that statement with an example or two. Can you give me one—a specific one?

5. This paper is great! Your teacher's sure to love it. I had Dr. Brunetti last semester, and he likes anything about World War II.

6. I always get confused between restrictive clauses and nonrestrictive clauses, too. I don't want to tell you the wrong thing, so let's look it up and check out the rules.

7. You keep writing "I think . . . ," but your teacher already knows that you're writing this paper and that the ideas are yours. Let's take this sentence. How can you rephrase it without using *I think*?

8. Your paper's due tomorrow and these notes are all you have? You should have written at least a draft by now.

9. You have a lot of misspellings and grammar problems. Let me read you this paragraph and show you what happens to me, as a reader, when I have to deal with so many mistakes.

10. You're arguing in support of stem cell research? I don't think I can work with you. I'm against it.

11. It doesn't really matter if English is not your home language. You have to fit in—you know, "When in Rome, do as the Romans do."

12. Do I ever sympathize! I used to make this same sort of mistake all the time. Then I learned what conjunctive adverbs are and how they work with semicolons and commas. Let's take this sentence where you use the word *however*, and I'll explain.

13. Why don't I just read your paper, and then I'll tell you what I think.

14. I'm not sure what your point is in this paragraph. Why don't you just tell me what it is you're trying to say?

15. I'm so glad you got me for a tutor. I took that class last semester and I have lots of ideas about that poem.

16. Let me play devil's advocate. You're arguing against fraternities, but I belong to one and there are lots of advantages.

17. You do have a problem if this paper's due this afternoon. Let's see what we can do, but I suggest you ask your teacher for an extension.

18. I'm really just here to help. Anything I tell you is just a suggestion. You can take my advice if you want, but you don't have to.

19. This looks like a really hard assignment. I don't quite understand it either. Professor Cunningham never does explain things very clearly. What do you think you're supposed to do?

20. Look, all you have to do to make this better is put in some more details. Here, when you look out of the window of the plane, talk about how tiny everything is. And with the food, say it tasted bland or delicious or whatever, then when you get to the landing part, say it was bumpy, smooth, loud, quiet, whatever it was. You'll have a good paper then.

21. I'm not an expert on documentation. You have a handbook. Just look it up.

22. I like your paper. It's really solid.

23. So this internship application asks you what you hope to accomplish through participating in it and how it relates to your academic and career goals. But, you know, everyone applying is smart and can benefit from it. So what about you makes it especially relevant? What do you expect to gain? What can you learn? And then, is there anything

about your background—your studies and experiences—that might be helpful to tell them more about you?

24. Clearly, you have some article usage problems, like here where you say "he was in hospital" and it should be "in THE hospital." English must not be your first language. Is it?

25. I also just had to write a twelve-page paper last week and thought I'd never finish! Where are you in the process? What do you think you can accomplish in the next three days before it's due?

26. Wait. What did Alex tell you to do? I totally disagree and his advice didn't seem to help your paper at all. In his defense, this is his first semester working in the writing center.

APPENDIX C

Role-playing Activities

Role-playing Tutoring Strategies

In pairs, role-play a "tutor" and "writer" starting a tutoring session. You can also role-play an online chat by logging on to two separate computers. The tutor can simply play himself or herself and practice the following techniques:

- Greeting a writer and building rapport
- Getting information from the writer
- Assessing the needs of the writer
- Setting the agenda and determining a plan of action
- Setting boundaries for the session
- Using active listening
- Wrapping up the session

"Writers" should adopt one of the personas listed in the next section but without telling the tutor which one.

Follow-up discussion should focus on the reactions and behavior of both tutor and "writer." How did you feel during the session? What made you comfortable or uncomfortable? What seemed to be successful, frustrating, helpful, and not helpful? How was body language evident in the session? How might the tutor have handled things differently? Though not necessary, it can be useful to videotape sessions for later viewing and analysis.

The "Writers"

1. You don't like the writing assignment you've been given—a comparison and contrast of two similar persuasive arguments for the same issue: revising the movie-rating system. It doesn't make sense to you.

Wouldn't it be better to look at two opposing opinions? Couldn't you pick your own topic? You also don't like your teacher. You think she's mean and withdrawn. If only she would just tell you what she wants, you could just do it. You're asking a tutor for help with your assignment, but what you really want is empathy and sympathy. Isn't this a terrible assignment? Isn't she a terrible teacher?

2. You've got your paper drafted and are fairly comfortable with it. You know that it probably needs to be tweaked a bit here and there to improve it, but that's about all. The teacher has said that he expects a strong introduction, and you know that yours could be a bit better. You also feel like your conclusion is too much of a rehash of what you just said. You're very open to suggestions and really expect that the tutor can give you some good advice.

3. You are a brand-new first-year student, you don't really know anyone very well yet, and so far college has been a far more scary experience than you'd thought it would be. You've been required to come to the writing center; otherwise, you would be in your dorm room, probably calling your parents or a close friend back home—again. You suspect that your writing skills are pretty good because you did well in high school, but you wonder how your writing compares with that of other first-year students. You hover near the door, unsure if you can muster the strength to enter the center. You barely speak above a whisper—if possible, not at all.

4. Fifteen years ago, you went to college for a couple of years, but you were unsure about what you wanted to do and finally quit. Now you're back in school and serious about getting a degree in education. But oh, that hiatus! You're very worried about your writing skills. Can you hold your own? What's the competition like? You're afraid you'll get a bad grade on this assignment. The paper is due in a week. You have brainstormed, outlined, and drafted. You suspect that there have been significant advances in approaches to writing over the past fifteen years, though you have no idea what those might be. You also have to pick up your children from school in an hour.

5. Swamped with several papers to write within the next two weeks, you have a ten-page history paper due today at noon. You got the research done for the history paper and finally sat down at 9:00 P.M. last night to write. At 5:00 A.M., you realized that you had good information, but you just weren't putting it together effectively. A couple of hours of sleep and now here you are, practically banging on the writing center's door and begging for help. In your sleep-deprived delirium, this paper has taken on extra importance. If you don't do well on it, you won't do well in the class. If you don't do well in the class, you won't do well in school. If you don't do well in school, you won't be able to get a job.

It's 8:55 right now; if you can get some help by 9:30, you can get home by 10:00, revise and edit by 11:00, then a half hour for the bibliography . . . where IS everybody who works here?

6. Teachers (and tutors) represent authority to you. After all, they know so much more than you do. You've been brought up not to question authority. Even if you don't understand what a tutor says, you won't ask questions or seek clarification. If the tutor asks you something, you smile and try quietly to cover up your lack of understanding. You expect that the tutor will take your paper, read it, and use his or her expertise to edit it during the session.

7. You're an economics graduate student, and you've just started the first semester of the MS program. You feel confident in your field but have struggled with writing for as long as you can remember. You just can't seem to translate your ideas and thoughts into a coherent paper. You are nervous about an upcoming research proposal and bring your draft to the writing center. You don't care if the person reviewing your proposal understands the content; you just want to make sure that you've expressed yourself clearly.

8. You're the kind of person who always has a thousand ideas bouncing around in your head at once. If someone asks you about subject A, you find some obscure relation to subject B and discuss that. (For example, in your paper praising tennis star Serena Williams, you leap to discussing your love of sports, especially soccer. Mention of your experiences on the high school team leads you into talk about an extracurricular activity, like the club sponsored by your favorite English teacher, which leads you to discuss what your favorite book was senior year.) You want help with this paper for your psychology class but just can't seem to focus on Jung's theories. You're likely to end up talking about anything but Jung in this session.

9. You are required to come to the writing center, and fulfilling this requirement is your main goal. You aren't much interested in the tutor's advice. The paper is due tomorrow, and you have the sketchiest of rough drafts, but you envision completing it easily in an hour or two this evening. You suspect that if you hand something in on time, you will receive a passing grade on it as well as in the class. At this moment, however, more than anything else, you want to be at home watching the basketball game. It's starting right about now. You have nothing against the tutor or the instructor, but you'll say anything to get the session over with.

10. You arrive at the writing center with a freshly printed copy of a paper for an English literature course. You are determined to get an A on this paper, so it must be letter-perfect. In taking advantage of this service for students, you assume that the tutor will scrutinize every

sentence, every word, and every punctuation mark. You expect nothing less and won't be satisfied until your paper is flawless.

11. You've always had difficulty with being organized and meeting deadlines. Your first paper in a first-year writing course is due this afternoon. As you sit with the tutor, you struggle to remember where in your bag you put your two-page, handwritten rough draft, and a search of your backpack yields only page two. When you talk to the tutor about the paper, you have difficulty remembering your topic and the points that you argued. As things become more confusing, you look to the tutor to save you from the mess you've created.

12. Everyone in your entomology class is required to visit the writing center with the final draft of a paper on how climate influences insect populations. In addition to the assignment sheet, the teacher has provided a lengthy list of general requirements that pertain to writing (no contractions, no jargon or slang, no misspellings, no incomplete sentences, no prepositions before commas or at ends of sentences, and so on). You're not sure if your paper explains the influence of climate adequately. You also want to make certain that your paper follows all of the requirements on the list.

13. You believe that you're a good writer, but you want to make sure the paper on Gilbert Stuart portraits for your art history course is as good as it can be. You've made an appointment at the writing center and are willing to listen to any suggestions that the tutor may have. You've noticed a sign in the center asking that cell phones be turned off, but you've ignored it. Several minutes into the session, your phone rings. You answer, and it's a friend whom you've been anxious to reach. After a moment, you excuse yourself and seek a more private place (perhaps around a corner or in the hall) where you can talk.

14. You're researching a historical figure for a course on local history. You have several sources (all websites), but as you work on the paper, you realize that you're depending heavily on one. As you explain to the tutor, you've searched the campus library website and the Internet and didn't find anything more. Is this okay? If not, how should you go about finding more detailed sources so that you are not relying on just one for the entire paper?

15. You are a transfer student. In order to be exempt from the first-year writing requirement at the college you now attend, you must submit a portfolio of work completed in a similar course at another school in another state. You want to be sure that your papers are acceptable, so you've made an appointment at the writing center. You assume that a tutor will be familiar with the first-year writing requirement at the school and that he or she can tell you if anything needs to be changed.

16. You and two other students have met to work on a group paper that's due in three hours. When a question arises about the correct format for documenting one entry, you disagree with the others in the group. Since the writing center is nearby, the three of you decide to ask an "expert." All the tutors are busy, so you interrupt a tutor with your "quick question."

17. You're writing a personal narrative about a difficult situation that you've encountered. You chose to describe your problems with a learning disability (or health problem), but because it's a significant issue for you, you find it difficult to write about. You want a decent grade on this paper, but you've resorted to being aloof and sometimes sarcastic because your frustration and anger get in the way as you write. Why do you have to explain everything? Shouldn't people just understand? Also, how "personal" should a personal narrative be? How will you know what to include and what to leave out?

18. You're getting started on a twenty-page paper for a graduate seminar in sociology. As an immigrant yourself, you want to explore how immigrants negotiate the territory between their old and new cultures. Your thinking is still fuzzy, but you believe that fictional works describe what happens well, while researchers tend to establish categories that leave gaps. What should you do? How should you proceed?

19. Your best language isn't English, but you've studied grammar and know the rules. Still, when you write, there are many mistakes. Your business teacher has failed your paper based on grammatical problems, but she says your content and organization are "quite good" and has allowed you to revise the paper. While you're grateful, you vaguely feel that she's discriminating against you because you are an international student. Still, you need a good grade on this paper because it's in your major.

20. You were assigned a group-written project in your sociology class. As usual with group projects, you felt that you did most of the work. What's more, the minor contributions from the rest of the group barely fit your style of writing. You want to see a tutor to help you better link the various sections and make them seem cohesive and written with one "voice."

Role-playing Tutoring Strategies in the Prewriting Stage

This role-playing exercise will help you practice active listening, facilitating, and using silence and wait time. Some of you will play a tutor or writer; others will observe the tutor's actions and words. (Role players might want to take a few minutes to jot down notes before beginning.) Following are descriptions of the responsibilities for each role.

WRITER. Assume that you need to write a letter or a well-composed e-mail message on one of the topics listed on pages 143–45 and that you are seeking a tutor's help to explore your ideas and to begin arranging them effectively. You will need to anticipate readers' objections to the ideas that you express in the letter. Use your imagination to come up with convincing arguments and objections. (Note that you do not have to write the letter or e-mail, as you are in the preliminary stages of writing.)

TUTOR. The writer is seeking your help with writing a letter or an e-mail. Your task is to help the writer:

- Explore persuasive arguments.
- Explore the audience's potential objections to those arguments and the writer's potential rebuttals to the objections.
- Begin planning an effective organization for the letter or e-mail.

At the same time, you must:

- Keep all of your ideas to yourself and make no contributions to the content or organization of the letter or e-mail.
- Pass no judgment on any of the ideas suggested by the writer. Ask questions that help the writer to focus and clarify ideas.

(Remember to practice active listening, facilitating, and using silence and wait time.)

OBSERVER(S). As the tutor works with the writer, look for examples of active listening, facilitative language, and silence or wait time. Make brief notes as you observe. (Your notes need not include a sentence's content, only enough to indicate that the tutor is being facilitative: "I can hear . . . ," "What do you think?" and so on.) You may want to complete a form like the one on page 26 for the session that you observe.

Your group might want to try different topics, trading roles as you move to a new topic. Each participant would thus get a chance to be a tutor, a writer, and an observer. After each session, group members should talk about how it felt to play the different roles. Observers should also share their impressions. What strategies did tutors use, and how effective were they? How could tutoring sessions have been improved?

LETTER OR E-MAIL TOPICS

1. Spring semester is nearly over, and your parents have been looking forward to having you at home for the summer. But you wish to live and work away from home, perhaps at the beach or near your school. Select the place where you want to live for the summer, and write an e-mail to your parents explaining your reasons; try to convince them that your living away from home is a good idea.

2. A number of students who use the writing center have indicated the need for additional writing center hours. Write a letter to the director either supporting or opposing extended hours.

3. You really enjoy using the writing center at your school, but you juggle school, a job, and a family. You wish that the writing center would offer an online feature. Write an e-mail to the director asking that an online, interactive component be added to the writing center. Be particular about what features you'd like to see and describe their usefulness to students like you.

4. As the parent of a young child, you find that attending classes poses some difficulties. Write a letter to the president of your school requesting a day-care facility for students' children. (If your school already has a day-care facility, ask that its hours be extended or assume that it is in danger of being closed and ask that it remain open.)

5. Write a letter to the president of your school asking for a change from letter grades to pass-fail designations (or the opposite if your school already offers pass-fail courses).

6. You are determined to participate in an exercise program while you are home for the summer, but you know that you would be more apt to stick with it if you had company. Write an e-mail advocating a particular exercise program (such as swimming, weight training, or aerobics) to a friend who will also be home, asking him or her to join you.

7. You have an opportunity to attend a three-day conference for writing tutors, but one of your professors frowns on students missing class. Write an e-mail to that professor explaining and justifying your request for an excused absence.

8. You and some friends have decided to travel for spring break. Write an e-mail to persuade your friends that swimming in Cancún would be better than skiing in Colorado. (Substitute other places and activities if you wish.)

9. Write a letter to the dean of your school suggesting that a specific campus program be started or continued. (Some suggestions: an orientation course for new students, a writing center, a math center, a study-abroad program, a particular internship.)

10. Your parents do not think that it is a good idea for you to have a car on campus, but increasingly you wish to have one. Write an e-mail to your parents explaining your reasons.

11. Your younger brother or sister is considering buying a computer but is not sure whether to choose a Mac or PC. Write an e-mail comparing the two options or explaining why one or the other is a better investment.

12. Your campus women's center is hosting a well-known speaker. As the student coordinator of the center, you need to arrange for facilities,

food, and security. But first, you need funding! Write a letter to the dean of student life requesting money for this event. Make sure that you explain the rationale for the amount of funds being requested.

13. Your school is considering adopting an honor pledge to be written and signed on examinations, papers, or other academic assignments. The pledge reads: "I pledge on my honor that I have not given or received any unauthorized assistance on this assignment/examination." Write a letter to the editor of your school newspaper supporting or opposing the idea.

14. You recently bought new portable speakers but are unhappy with the overall quality of the product. Write an email of complaint to the manufacturer, and ask for a refund.

15. You belong to an organization that is seeking to attract and better serve new members. You believe that a formal mentoring program would allow seasoned members to share their expertise with newer ones. Draft a proposal explaining the needs for and benefits of a mentoring arrangement.

Role-playing Different Tutoring Situations

Read through each of the following three scenarios twice. (If you are using this guide as part of a tutoring class, you and other tutors may want to act out the different parts.) As you do the preliminary read, consider the following questions:

- How is the tutor probably feeling? How do you know? What verbal and nonverbal clues indicate his or her feelings?
- How is the writer probably feeling? How do you know? What verbal and nonverbal clues can you find?

As you go through the scenarios the second time, consider the following questions:

- What are the tutor's expectations?
- What are the writer's expectations?
- What are some other ways in which the tutor might have handled the situation?

These scenarios provide excellent material for group discussion, and you can use the preceding questions as departure points.

Scenario 1

Tutor: Hi! [Smiles.] My name's Lars. We can just sit over here. Grab that chair. [They sit.] What can I do for you?

Writer: Well, I'm Stefan, and I have this paper [hands it to tutor], and, uh, my teacher said I had to come here and, uh, get some help 'cause my last paper ... [looks down] was a D.

Tutor: Then maybe we should just begin by reading through it out loud. Do you want to read, or would you rather I did?

Writer: [Motions to tutor and mutters "You," then folds arms across chest and gazes off into space.]

Tutor: [Begins reading but is clearly having trouble. Stumbles over words and stops several times to clarify a word. As tutor reads, writer occasionally sighs, taps fingers on desk and feet on floor.]. I'm sorry—it's just that I don't seem to be able to read this aloud in the style and voice you intended. It would probably be easier if you read your paper to me. Would you mind?

Writer: [Hesitates.] Naw, I guess not. [Reads about halfway down page, suddenly stops and slams hand down on desk and looks at tutor.] I really don't see the point of this.

Tutor: Well, it's just easier for me to tutor, to help you with your paper, if I hear what you've written.

Writer: [Waits a few moments, then tosses paper in front of tutor and speaks in a demanding way.] Can't you just check it and fix it?

Tutor: When you come here and ask to have a paper proofread, the receptionist will tell you that the writing center isn't a proofreading service. It's a tutoring service. You can have a tutor like me look at your paper with you and discuss your problems and then try to show you how to correct them. We don't just correct students' papers!

Writer: [Annoyed.] Well, I was told that you did! My friend said I could just have a tutor correct my grammar.

Tutor: [Firmly.] Well, I'm sorry. I don't tutor that way. [Silence.]

Tutor: If you want me to continue reading through . . .

Writer: [Cuts tutor off, snatches paper away from tutor, looks quickly at watch.] I just don't have time for this. Nothing against you, but I just don't have time for this. [Collects papers quickly and gets up.]

Tutor: [Stares in disbelief.] I'm really sorry. I just don't tutor that way.

Writer: That's okay. It's nothing against you. [Walks out.]

Scenario 2

[The tutor is sitting at a computer, and begins a synchronous online chat with a writer.]

Tutor: Hi! I'm Maryam. What can I do to help you?

Writer: I don't know if you can. I only have a draft of a paper, or the start of one. I'm Lee, by the way. Not sure what to do. Just wrote some stuff down. Parts of it just don't sound right.

Tutor: What's your assignment?

Writer: A book review for history. Nothing specific, really, just a review. The book's *Long Walk to Freedom: The Autobiography of Nelson Mandela.*

Tutor: ☺ Great! Have you ever written a book review before? Do you know what you're supposed to include?

Writer: Sort of. I think I'm supposed to give my opinion.

Tutor: Something like that. What you're supposed to do is evaluate it and use evidence from the book—like quotes and examples and references—to back up what you say. So tell me some of your ideas. What did you like about the book? Take your time; I'll be here!

[The cursor blinks for a few minutes.]

Writer: Well, I don't really know. Have you read it? What do you think about it?

Tutor: Nope, haven't read it. Sorry! Why don't you just tell me some of your ideas? That will be a good starting point.

Writer: If you haven't read the book, I don't see how you can help me.

Tutor: I understand your frustration! But I think I can still help. In fact, it's probably better that I haven't read it. You'll have to explain things to me, and that'll help you sort out your ideas. If you just tell me what some of your ideas are, we can chat about them and I can help you think them through a bit. I do that all the time here.

Writer: I just don't see how that will work. I mean, if you haven't read the book . . . ☹

Tutor: Yes, but you have, so it's really not a problem. I can tell that this is frustrating for you, but I can help.

[The cursor blinks again for a minute or so.]

Tutor: You have read the book, haven't you?

Writer: Most of it. I mean, it's really long, and I don't know. I can't get into it.

Tutor: Well, maybe you could tell me about the parts you have read, and we can at least start working from there. You said you wrote some things down. Can you e-mail me or copy and paste what you do have? It'll be a good start . . .

Scenario 3

[The tutor is sitting. The writer sits down beside the tutor.]

Tutor: [Cheerfully.] Hi! I'm Willem. What are you working on?

Writer: Oh, hi. I'm Marlene. I have to do a five-page paper analyzing this poem. It's due tomorrow morning—early. I don't know. It's really hard to do that stuff, don't you think? Why do teachers give assignments like this, anyway?

Tutor: Well, they do. And, I know, sometimes it's just not easy.

Writer: [Hesitates.] Uh, I haven't really started it yet. Because I can't figure out what I'm supposed to do. Here's the poem and here's the assignment sheet. [Hands poem and assignment sheet to tutor.] What should I do? I really don't understand what the teacher wants.

Tutor: [Glances at papers.] Oh, I know that poem. [Looks up.] Did the teacher explain anything about the paper in class?

Writer: Yeah, we're supposed to read the poem and analyze it, but I just don't know what she wants. [Looks baffled.] How do you analyze a poem?

Tutor: Well, let's see what the assignment sheet says.

Writer: [Sighs.] I can't figure out the assignment sheet. It's so confusing to read. Can you read it and tell me what I'm supposed to do?

Tutor: [Hesitates, glances at it, and then smiles.] Sure, let me read it. It's short. [Reads it over.] Oh, here it is! At the bottom it tells you what to do.

Writer: Oh, I didn't read that far. I got confused by the beginning stuff, with all those terms. The teacher never really explains anything to us. I hate that.

Tutor: Well, let's see if we can sort it out. The poem . . .

Writer: [Interrupts.] Don't you just hate when teachers don't tell you what they want? If they just would tell me, I think I would be able to write it. [Pauses and grins.] So, you figured out the assignment? What am I supposed to do?

Tutor: [Pauses.] You know, what I'm hearing is that you're frustrated because you don't know what to do and the paper's due tomorrow. Let's look at the assignment sheet together. You can tell me which parts confuse you, and I can try to explain . . .

Writer: [Angrily.] Look, I have to pass this class and I have to do the paper to pass it. Just tell me what to do! You know the poem and you know what I'm supposed to do . . .

Tutor: [Firmly but politely.] Yes, but I can't do the paper for you. I can help you, but it's your paper.

Writer: I know, I know, I know, but what am I supposed to do? It's due tomorrow! [Emphatically.] I hate poetry!

Tutor: Well, I'm trying to help, but . . .

Writer: Yeah, but it's so late. Just tell me what to say! Aren't you supposed to help me?

Tutor: I can help you, but if you don't want to do your share of the work, there's not much I can do.

Writer: [Grabs the papers.] Yeah, well, thanks for nothing. I should have figured you tutors would be just like the teacher.

APPENDIX D

Outside Tutoring and Editing Jobs

Often, people or companies contact writing centers or individuals in search of private tutors or editors. The following are some suggestions for dealing with prospective employers.

Negotiating the Professional Relationship

You are a professional who is being paid not only for the work you do but also for your experience, professional training, and level of education. Because you already tutor in a writing center, for a company, or privately, you have a certain amount of professional credence. Don't sell yourself short!

Pay is probably not the first matter you want to discuss—not because it is bad form, but because in order to discuss pay intelligently and fairly, you should know certain details about the job.

QUESTIONS ABOUT TUTORING JOBS

- How much preparation time will be required (for planning, gathering materials, talking to instructors, and so on)?
- Are you responsible for planning the tutoring agenda, or will it be set by an outside source (teachers, SAT preparation books, and so on)?
- Will you be reading papers or reviewing exercises? (The former usually takes more time.)
- How often will you be meeting with the writer? For what duration will you be meeting with the writer (throughout the semester, over the summer, etc.)? Will you be meeting in-person or online? Is travel involved?
- What is the writer's skill level? Does she have any special needs or problems?

149

Jon Kudelka.

- Has the writer worked with a tutor before? What was and was not accomplished?
- What are the major goals of the person(s) hiring you?

QUESTIONS ABOUT EDITING JOBS

- What, precisely, does the employer expect you to do? Some people may say that they simply need help "proofreading" when they actually want you to do major rewriting. You will need to determine if the job entails copyediting (tightening and clarifying sentences, fixing grammatical errors, and so on) or major revision (basically, rewriting significant portions of the text). Ask to be sent several pages of text so you can assess the level and amount of work that will be involved.
- How will the editing be done—by hand on a manuscript or digitally at a computer?
- Will you be expected to use your own computer, paper, or other supplies?
- How much freedom will you be given? Can you edit on your own, or will you have to work closely with the writer?
- What sort of timetable does the writer expect? Does she want you to send portions as you complete them or the entire text upon completion?

Negotiating Pay

To help determine what to charge, talk to others who also tutor or edit privately. What do their jobs entail with respect to the details listed above, and how much do they charge? You may also call or visit tutoring or editing agencies in your geographic area to learn the going rate.

Before you accept an editing job, make sure that both you and your employer are in agreement about whether you will be paid according to the time you spend on the text or according to the total number of pages. Some editors charge per hour; others charge a certain amount per page. The latter allows you and the person hiring you to estimate the costs more easily. Whether tutoring or editing, arrange to be paid at regular and frequent intervals (for example, after each tutoring session). Do not allow charges to accumulate. Keep a record of the payment schedule. If the client pays in person, show him that you are keeping the record up-to-date by taking it out each time you are paid and noting the payment. If the client pays online, be sure to email acknowledgement of the payment. Another option is to ask the client to pay ahead of time for a specified amount of work, a method that works well if you are working online and not meeting with the client face-to-face. When you reach the agreed-upon limit, the two of you can negotiate for more time and money.

Negotiating Time

- **For tutoring:** In tutoring situations, keep track of time, and try not to go over the limit; if you do, people will tend to expect that you will work longer for them regularly. You cannot expect people to pay for your preparation time, so factor this time into the per-hour rate agreed upon. You may, for example, read a literary work or spend time preparing activities beforehand, and you should be compensated for your work. Also, people do not usually pay for travel time, so take this into account as well.
- **For editing:** Keep meticulous track of time. The clock should be running from the moment you pick up the work until the time you put it down for the day. If you find that the work is taking more time than you thought, confer with the client.

Arranging Meeting Space

If you are tutoring someone in person, plan to meet at a public place, like a library, a study room on campus, or a coffee shop. Public places, rather than someone's home, are safer and often more conducive to getting work done. They tend to offer fewer distractions for the person being tutored, and they provide you with greater control over the environment. If you are tutoring someone online, be sure you first vet the platform you plan on using and then build in time for any necessary training or practice prior to the first tutoring session.

Planning for the Long Term

- **For tutoring:** Will you be expected to work toward certain goals (such as helping a student pass an exam)? How much time do you have to meet those goals, and how much responsibility do you have for their successful completion?
- **For editing:** Will you be expected to work toward certain deadlines? What are they? Will there be rush periods?

Index